L

Everyma

C000257648

CONTENTS

Welcome to Lisbon!

This opening fold-out contains a general map of Lisbon to help you visualise the 6 large districts discussed in this guide, and 4 pages of valuable information, handy tips and useful addresses.

Discover Barcelona through 6 districts and 6 maps

A Belém

B Alcântara / Lapa / Estrela / Rato

C São Sebastião / Saldanha / Monsanto

D Restauradores / Bairro Alto / Chiado

E Baixa / Alfama / Castelo

F Graça / Alfama / Parque das Nações

For each district there is a double-page of addresses (restaurants – listed in ascending order of price – pubs, bars, music venues and shops) followed by a fold-out map for the relevant area with the essential places to see (indicated on the map by a star ★). These places are by no means all that Lisbon has to offer but to us they are unmissable. The grid-referencing system (**A** B2) makes it easy for you to pinpoint addresses quickly on the map.

Transport and hotels in Lisbon

The last fold-out consists of a transport map and 4 pages of practical information that include a selection of hotels.

Thematic index

Lists all the sites and addresses featured in this guide.

HARBORS AND RIVER LINKS

→ Tel. 21 340 4539
*Departures Mon-Sat 9am
Price 12.45 €/3 hrs (with
1 drink included)*
Discover the city's districts
and their hidden treasures.

MARKETS

Food market
Feira da Ribeira Nova (**B** E3)
→ *Av. 24 de Julho
Mon-Sat 6am–2pm*
Fruit and vegetables,
fish, meat and flowers.
**Mercado municipal
24 de Julho (D** C6)
→ *Cais do Sodré
Fruit and vegetable
market: Mon-Sat 7am–2pm
Flower market: Mon, Wed,
Fri 7.30-10pm; Tue, Thu 3-7pm*
Lively atmosphere in the
former fish market.
Flea market
Feira da Oeiras
→ *Jardim Municipal
Last Sunday of the month.*
Vast market selling second-
hand goods.

SHOPPING

Opening times
*Mon-Fri 9am–1pm, 3-7pm;
Sat 9am–1pm for shops.
Daily 10am–midnight for
shopping centers.*
Sales
Twice yearly: Jan 15- Feb 15
and Aug 15- Sep 15.
Discounts
Lisboa Shopping Card
→ *2.50 €/1 day, 4.50 €/3 days*
Five to 20% discount in
over 200 shops.
Shopping malls
C.C. Mouraria (**E** B2)
→ *Martim Moniz*
For a quick trip around the
world – African, Indian and
Chinese shops.
Saldanha Atrium (**C** F3)
→ *Praça Duque de Saldanha*
For modern, leading fashion
brands.
C.C. Colombo
→ *Mº Colégio Militar*
500 shops, cinemas,
go-carting and bowling.

Lisbon stylists
José António Tenente (**D** D4)
→ *Travessa do Carmo 8*
Comfortable, elegant
clothes by a former...
architect.
Iznougud
→ *Av. Almirante Reis 113,
C.C. Portugália*
Top-quality clothes by
Portuguese designers, and
a good selection of London
imports.

RESTAURANTS

Opening times
Breakfast: all morning
(coffee with a sandwich
pastry, or cod fritter).
Lunch (noon–2.30pm)
and dinner (8–10pm)
good portions served with
potatoes or rice; don't
hesitate to ask for a half-
portion (*meia dose*).
Service and tipping
Service is always included
in the price. Optional tip
(10%).

ARCHITECTURE

Moorish style
Lose yourself in the **Alfam**
Lisbon's medina. Or follo
the touradas in the **Camp**
Pequeno (**C** F1) in neo-
Moorish style.
Manueline style
Introduced in the reign o
King Manuel I (1495–152
this late-Gothic style
incorporates lavish
ornamentation and sea
motifs inspired by the Ag
of Discoveries. **Mosteiro
dos Jerónimos, Torre de
Belém (A** A4).
Pombaline style
After the earthquake
of 1755, the Marquês de
Pombal, minister to King
João I, rebuilt the **Baixa
(E** B4) in a checkerboard
pattern with understated
buildings. This first
example of rationalist
town- planning was geete
with admiration across
Europe.
Contemporary style
Since the return of
democracy, Lisbon has
been at the leading edge
the avant-garde.
Parque das Nações (F E3
Modernist buildings,
a suspension bridge,
a futurist tower and a cab
car along the Tagus, on th
site of Expo 1998.

AZULEJOS

Introduced by the Arabs i
Spain in the 16th century,
these thick painted faïenc
tiles adorn Lisbon's house
and monuments. Used
widely on façades after th
fire of 1755 to protect the
buildings from flames.
Fábrica Sant'Ana (D C5)
→ *Rua do Alecrim, 95*
Tel. 21 342 2537

THE TAGUS

CITY PROFILE

- Capital of Portugal
- River: the Tagus (Rio Tejo)
- 611,000 inhabitants over 52 square miles
- Temperature: 52° F in February, 72° C in July; humid from December to March

VIEW FROM LE MIRADOURO DE SANTA LUZIA

AFRICAN LISBON

Cape Verdean and Mozambican stalls, restaurants and dance halls in the district of São Bento, the stronghold of the Portuguese African community.
Associação de Cabo Verde (C E4**)**
→ *Duque de Palmela, 2*
Information on activities in the Cape Verdean community.
Radio RDP-Africa (C C4**)**
→ *Av. E. Duarte Pacheco, 26 / 101.5 FM*
Free concerts Wed, 6pm
African day of culture
→ *May 16*

EURO (€)

At the time of writing the new European currency has not been officially launched. Check the Euro exchange rate with your bank/travel agent before departure.

TOURIST INFORMATION

Portuguese Tourist Office (D D2**)**
→ *Praça dos Restauradores*
Tel. 21 346 3314
Mon-Sat 9am–8pm; Sun and public hols 9am–6pm
→ *Airport Office*
Tel. 21 844 6473
Hotel reservations and tourist information.
Lisboa Welcome Center (E B5**)**
→ *Praça do Comércio*
Tel. 21 031 2810
Daily 9am–8pm
Tourist information in English and French

about Lisbon and the surrounding area.

GREEN SPACES

Parc Eduardo VII (C E4**)**
→ *Daily 9am–5.30pm (4.30pm from Oct-March)*
Vast French-style garden, opened in 1902, whose 50 acres include tennis courts and a sports center.
Jardim botânico Aduja (A C2**)**
→ *Calçada da Ajuda*
Thu-Tue 10am–5pm
The oldest botanical garden in the country (1768), designed by the Marquês de Pombal.
Jardim da Estrela (B D2**)**
→ *Calçada da Estrela*
Daily 7am–midnight
Exotic plants and romantic winding paths. Bandstand in summer, café-terrace and restaurant.
Tapada das Necessidades (B C3**)**
→ *Calçada das*

Necessidades
Mon-Fri 9am–6pm
The oldest cactus garden in Europe.

SIGHTSEEING WITH A DIFFERENCE

Streetcars (Éléctricos)
Lines 12, 18, 25, 26
→ *Streetcar maps and tickets from Carris kiosks.*
Take the most popular mode of transport in Lisbon; four historic lines are still in service.
Circuito das Colinas
→ *Journey time 1½ hrs, price 15 €. Tickets from point of departure (Praça do Comércio). Connection with lines 25 & 28 included.*
Tour of Lisbon's seven hills in a stylish red streetcar, includes commentary.
Cable cars
Vasco da Gama Cable Car
(F F4**)**
→ *Mon-Fri 11am–7pm; Sat-Sun 10am–8pm*

2.50 € single; 5 € return
Spectacular trip above the Rio Tejo and the Parque das Nações (Oceanário to the Torre Vasco da Gama).
Ferries
Gray Line
→ Tel. 21 882 0347
April-Oct Price 15 €
Leaves from T. do Paço
Step aboard the Gray Line for a two-hour cruise on the Sea of Straw.
Crossing the Tagus
Transtejo Transportes SA
→ Tel. 21 310 3131
Crossings every 10 mins–1 hr until 10pm.
Price 0.50-1.50 €.
Tickets from the stations.
This ferry stops at a number of cities around the bay. The trip provides a wonderful way to relax and affords magnificent views over Lisbon from the south bank (cf. map of landing stages above).
Guided tours
Walking around Lisbon

Welcome to Lisbon!

A Belém

B Alcântara / Lapa / Estrela / Rato

C São Sebastião / Saldanha / Monsanto

D Restauradores / Bairro Alto / Chiado

E Baixa / Alfama / Castelo

F Graça / Alfama / Parque das Nações

AV. DAS NAÇÕES UNIDAS

LUZ

AV. MAR. TEIXEIRA REBELO

ELIAS GARCIA

AV. GENERAL NORTON DE MATOS

AVENIDA LUSÍADA

RUA CONDE DE ALMOSTER

C JARDIM ZOOLÓGICO

BOA VISTA

PARQUE FLORESTAL DE MONSANTO

ALTO DA SERAFINA

A5

ESTRADA DO PENEDO

A5

B CAMPO DE OURIQUE

AV. DA PONTE

AV. DE CEUTA

AVENIDA DAS DESCOBERTAS

CARAMÃO

PALÁCIO NACIONAL DA AJUDA

CALÇADA DA AJUDA

AJUDA

SANTO AMARO

PALÁCIO REAL D. NECESSIDADES

ALCÂNTARA

AV. INFANTE SANTO

AV. VINTE E

AV. DO RESTELO

MOSTEIRO DOS JERÓNIMOS

Pr. A. de Albuquerque

AVENIDA DA ÍNDIA

AV. DA PONTE

PONTE 25 DE ABRIL

AVENIDA DA ÍNDIA

TORRE DE BELÉM

A

MIRADOUROS

Vantage points for breathtaking views over the city and its river.

Senhora do Monte (E D1**)**
→ *Rua S. do Monte (Graça) / streetcar n° 28*
Cavalcade of boats up and down the Tagus and Lisbon's hills.

Santa Luzia (E D4**)**
→ *Alfama streetcar n°28*
View over the Alfama and the Tagus beneath the bougainvilleas.

São Pedro de Alcântara (D C3**)**
→ *Bairro Alto Elevador da Glória*
The city center and the 'lower city' in one go.

ELEVADOR DA GLÓRIA

corrida, without any killing.

MUSEUMS

Opening times
Tue 2–6pm; Wed-Sun 10am–6pm. Closed Sun, public hols (national museums)
Tue-Sun 10am–1pm, 2–5pm. Closed Sun, public hols (other museums)
Admission price
→ *1–2.50 € depending on the museum*
Discount
Lisboa Card
→ *11 €/1 day, 18 €/2 days, 23 €/3 days. From tourist kiosks and tourist offices.*
Unlimited use of subway and Carris transport, free entry to 25 museums and monuments.

CALENDAR OF EVENTS

Senhor dos Passos
→ *March 6*
Procession between the Igreja da Saude and the Igreja da Graça.

Book fair
→ *mid-May/mid-June*
Open-air book stalls in the Praça do Comércio and Rua Augusta.

Festas dos Santos Populares
→ *June 1-30*
Shows, fireworks, sporting events, a circus and widespread celebrations on the night of June 12 (Eve of Santo Antonio).

Lisboa mexe-me
→ *mid-July/mid-August*
Open-air shows in the old districts.

TELEPHONE

Codes
UK/US to Lisbon
→ *00/011 351 + phone n°*
Lisbon to UK / USA
→ *00 44/00 1 + phone n°*
Telephone cards
→ *Cards of 50, 120 or 200 units from Post Offices,*

tobacconists, newsstands
Coin-operated phones: telephone and bankers' cards accepted.
Useful numbers
Police
→ *Tel. 21 346 6141*
Emergencies
→ *Tel. 115*
Loss or theft
→ *Rua Capelo, 13*
Tel. 21 346 6141
(international police; open 24 hrs)

INTERNET

Internet sites
General information
→ *www.portugalinsite.pt*
→ *www.atl-turismolisboa.pt*
Cultural sites
→ *www.lazer.publico.pt*
Cybercafé
Cyber Chiado
→ *Largo do Picadeiro, 12*
Mon-Fri 11–1.30am;
Sat 2.30pm–midnight
3.50 €/hr
Arts and Internet Center.

FURTHER AFIELD

Beaches
Costa do Caparica
→ *Take bus 75 from M° Campo Grande*
Venture a little way from the concrete landscape of the seaside resort of Caparica to find beaches and dunes stretching as far as the eye can see.
Costa do Sol
→ *By train from Cais do Sodré (every 20 mins)*
Beaches frequented by the Lisboans.
Sintra
→ *Estação do Rossio*
A site listed by Unesco.
Palacio Nacional
→ *Tel. 21 910 6840*
The only royal residence dating from the Middle Ages. Remarkable Shield Room with a collection of azulejos.
Palacio Nacional da Pena
→ *Tel. 21 910 5340*
Flamboyant building in romantic neo-medieval style (1840). The last residence of the royal family.
Parque Natural de Sintra-Cascais
→ *Train for Cascais (from Cais do Sodré) then bus 403-405-415*
The westernmost stretch of European coast. Wind-scoured cliffs and moor at Cabo da Roca, sandy creeks at Guincho.
Queluz
Palacio Nacional
→ *Tel. 21 435 0039*
Cais do Sodré.
Departs every 15 mins
A baroque, neoclassical palace known as the 'little Versailles' (18th c.). Lavishly decorated Throne Room. Regular ballets and concerts.

ELEVADORES

Refers both to elevators and funicular railroads.
→ *Carris tickets valid*
Service daily 7am–11pm
Elevador da Bica (D A1)
To reach the district of Calhariz.
Elevador da Glória (D B5)
From the Praça dos Restauradores to the Bairro Alto.
Elevador do Lavra (D D2)
The oldest urban funicular in the world (1884).
Elevador de Santa Justa (E A4)
A spectacular metal tower linking the Baixa with the Chiado.

TELEPHONE KIOSK

SANTA LUZIA STALL

---

scounts
boa Restaurant Card
5 €/person; 7 €/2 people;
o €/2 adults + 2 children
der 14
to 15 % discount in over
restaurants in the center.
d 72 hrs.

ing out
sas de pasto: Simple,
xpensive meals, such as
z de marisco (a rice and
food stew).
cas: A Portuguese
itution: a bistro serving
e-cooked cuisine. Ask
he dish of the day
to do dia).
rraqueiras: Grilled
cialities, such as frango
ado, grilled chicken
ab.
vejarias: Popular beer
s serving seafood, fresh
and draft beers.

OWS

ervations
rvations and ticket

sales for the latest concerts and plays etc can be bought from ABEP and FNAC.
ABEP (D D2)
→ *Praça dos Restauradores*
Tel. 21 347 5824.
Daily 9am–10pm
FNAC
→ *Colombo Shopping Center*
M° Colégio Militar / Liz
Tel. 21 711 4237
Daily 10am–midnight
Information about shows
Público
→ *Daily from newsstands*
Calendar of exhibitions, movies and shows around the city.
Agenda Cultural
→ *Free monthly magazine from tourist offices*
A listings magazine with the month's cultural events.
Radio Paris-Lisbonne
→ *90.4 FM*
A cultural radio station, in French and Portuguese.
Theaters/opera houses
Teatro Taborda (E C3)
→ *Costa do Castelo, 75*

Tel. 21 888 1718
Shows by independent theater companies, below the buttresses of the Castelo.
Teatro Nacional de São Carlos (D D5)
→ *Rua Serpa Pinto, 9*
Tel. 21 346 8408
Ballet, drama and concerts in a great rococo auditorium.
Art centers
Ballet, concerts (from classical music to variety shows) and theater, in one of the city's cultural forums.
Fundação Gulbenkian (C E2)
→ *Av. de Berna, 45*
Tel. 21 793 5131
Centro Cultural de Belém (A B4)
→ *Praça do Império*
Tel. 21 361 2400
Culturgest
→ *Rua Arco do Cego*
Tel. 21 790 5155
Movies
Cinemateca Portuguesa

(D B1)
→ *Rua B. Salgueiro, 39*
Tel. 21 354 6529
Old films (original language) and Portuguese avant-garde. Movie museum and library.

SPORTS AND PASTIMES

Football
Estádio da Luz
→ *M° Colégio Militar, bus 44*
Tel. 21 726 6053 / Price 2.50–30 € Aug–June : Sun
Benfica's famous stadium.
Estádio José de Alvalade
→ *M° Campo Grande, bus 1, 36 / Tel. 21 758 9021*
Price 2.50–30 €
Home of the second local team, the Sporting.
Touradas
Campo Pequeno (C F1)
→ *Av. da Republica*
Tel. 21 793 2442
May–Sep: Thu 10pm
Price 10–40 €
Portuguese version of the

Praça de
Malaca

PLANETÁRIO
GULBENKIAN

★
L. dos
Jerónimos

PALÁCIO
DE BELÉM

RUA D. FRANCISCO DE ALMEIDA

Praça
de Diu

L. DE ALMEIDA

MUSEU
DOS

RUA SÃO FRANCISCO XAVIER

★
MUSEU DA
MARINHA

Pr. do
Império

MOSTEIRO DOS
JERÓNIMOS/
MUSEU NACIONAL
DE ARQUEOLÓGIA

R. DE BELÉM

MUSEU
DOS

BELÉM

Pr. A. de
Albuquerque

AV. DA TORRE DE BELÉM

RUA B. DIAS

★
FONTE
LUMINOSA

CENTRO CULTURAL
DE BELÉM

AVENIDA DA ÍNDIA

AVENIDA DE BRASÍLIA

ESTAÇÃO
DE BE

4

AVENIDA DE BRASÍLIA

DOCA DE BOM
SUCESSO

★
MUSEU NACIONAL
DE ARTE POPULAR

★ PADRÃO DOS
DESCOBRIMENTOS

TORRE DE
★ BELÉM   A

B

C

MUSEU DA MARINHA

CENTRO CULTURAL DE BELÉM

★ **Palácio Nacional
da Ajuda** (**A** C2)
→ *Calçada da Ajuda*
Tel. 21 363 7095
*Mon-Tue, Thu-Sun 10am–
5pm. Closed public hols*
The rooms of this former
19th-century royal palace
contain decorative arts
(15th-20th century),
silverware and jewelry
(Portuguese crown jewels).
★ **Museu Nacional
dos Coches** (**A** C3)
→ *Praça A. de Albuquerque*
Tel. 21 361 0850
Tue-Sun 10am–5.30pm
Closed public hols
An impressive collection
of carriages, berlins,
barouches and period

sedan chairs (17th-19th
century), kept since 1905
in the former riding hall
of the Belém Royal Palace.
Paintings, gilding, carvings,
allegories of the glory of
Portugal's conquests and
discoveries offer a trip
back in time to the reign of
the Portuguese monarchs.
★ **Jardim do Ultramar**
(**A** C3)
→ *Largo dos Jerónimos*
Tue-Sun 10am–5pm
Closed public hols
In June, the colonial garden
is invaded by the perfume
of jasmine. Palms, ficus,
eucalyptus and other
plants brought here in the
early 20th century recall

the country's colonial past.
★ **Mosteiro dos
Jerónimos/Museu
Nacional de Arqueológia**
(**A** B3)
→ *Praça do Império*
Tel. 21 362 0034 (monastery)
Tel. 21 362 0000 (museum)
*Monastery: Tue-Sun 10am–
5pm / Museum: Tue 2–6pm;
Wed-Sun 10am–6pm*
Closed public hols
One of the finest examples
of Manueline architecture,
this monastery is late Gothic
in style with sculptural
motifs inspired by the Age
of Discoveries. With money
from the spice trade,
Manuel I had this building
constructed in 1502 to

honour the Portugu
monarchy. The mon
is decorated with a
number of orname
as floral motifs (bu
grapes, leaves, pin
sea motifs (ropes, e
shells) and Renaiss
grotesques. Make s
see: the side porta
masterpiece by on
greatest master sto
masons; the breat
star-shaped vault o
church (N. Chante
1516); and the tom
Vasco de Gama an
Camões (Almeida
chapel). The muse
wing) contains po
weapons and jewe

JARDIM DO ULTRAMAR

CADA DO
JARDIM DO ULTRAMAR

CALÇADA DO GALVÃO

R. DOS JERÓNIM
RUA QUINZE

DE ALCOLENA

R. GEN. M. ANDRM
R. DAS
AJUD
A AJUD

TRA
R. DAS MERCÊS

CALÇADA DA AJUDA
R. DO JARDIM BOTÂNICO

JARDIM BOTÂNICO

CALÇADA DO GALVÃO

R. DAS PEDREIRAS
R. DAS FERRAS

RUA GONÇALVES ZARCO

ESTÁDIO DO RESTELO

RUA PÊRO DA COVILHÃ

RUA DE ALENQUER

RUA PÊRO DA COVILHÃ

MUSEU DE ETNOLOGIA

RUA D.C. DE BRAGANÇA

RUA ANTÓNIO DE SALDANHA

ALTO DA AJUDA

CEMITÉRIO DA AJUDA

AVENIDA DA ILHA DA MADEIRA

R. DIOGO DE TEIVE

R. GONÇALO VELHO CABRAL

RUA DIOGO DE SILVES

R. DAS AÇUCENAS
R. TRÊS

SOCO

R. DOS MARCOS

ESTR. DE CASELAS

RUA ANTÃO GONÇALVES

RUA GREGÓRIO LOPES

AVENIDA DAS DESCOBERTAS

RUA COLÉGIO DE SÃO JOSÉ

AV. HELEN KELLER

ESTR. DE P. TEIXEIRA

R. JACINTO

AV. DR. MÁRIO MOUTINHO

R. CÍNICO

AV. DOS BOMBEIROS

ESTR. DE CASELAS

RUA P.
RUA P.

ESTRADA DOS MARCOS

ESTRADA DE QUELUZ

RUA BASTOS

RUA WHITE FUR

B.º CARAMÃO

A

R. DO GRAVATO

PALÁCIO NACIONAL DA AJUDA

MUSEU NACIONAL DOS COCHES

JARDIM DO ULTRAMAR

Stretching along the northwest bank of the Tagus, the *bairro* (district) of Belém celebrates the Age of Discoveries and Portugal's great explorers. Monuments to the golden age of Portuguese navigation stand next to masterpieces of Manueline architecture along embankments lined with parks and promenades. Center stage is the modern Centro de Belém, an attractive stone complex with Mediterranean terraces, bearing witness to the cultural dynamism of the Portuguese capital: two concert venues, a bookshop, a museum, and shops in the nerve center of the district.

XI HU   A COMMENDA

RESTAURANTS

Cervejaria O Prado
(A C3)
→ *Rua da Junqueira*
Tel. 21 364 2412
Daily 9am–midnight
This restaurant has large picture windows giving onto the street and several canteen-style tables where you can sample an *açorda de marisco* (soup made from bread and seafood), seafood rice, grilled meat or fish. Homemade desserts.
À la carte 7.50-10 €.

Xi Hu (A C3)
→ *Rua de Belém, 95–99*
Tel. 21 362 3322
Daily 10am–10.30pm
All the great classics of Chinese cuisine (assorted soups, chicken, beef or fish in sauce), keenly priced, in an attractive long dining room. Tourist menu 9 €, 10 € à la carte.

Rosa dos Mares (A C3)
→ *Rua de Belém, 110*
Tel. 21 362 1811
Tue-Sun noon–11pm
Although there are countless tourist restaurants on this street, you can't go wrong with this one. Cooked seafood (grilled swordfish, prawn curry) and the house specialty: seafood rice (for two people).

Delightful little terrace overlooking the street and two bright dining rooms with ocher tiles.
À la carte 15 €.

Vela Latina (A A4)
→ *Doca do Bom Sucesso*
Tel. 21 301 7118
Mon-Sat 12.30–3pm, 8–11.30pm
A huge restaurant with a pleasant garden area between the Padrão dos Descobrimentos and the Torre de Belém. Excellent traditional Portuguese cuisine: platters of ultra-fresh seafood, grilled fish and game (partridges in wine sauce).
À la carte 15-17.45 €.

A Commenda (A B4)
→ *Centro Cultural de Belém, 1400.* Tel. 21 364 8561
Mon-Sat 12.30–3.30pm, 7.30–11pm; Sun 11.30am–3pm
This restaurant provides a sophisticated and romantic setting for a first-class marriage of Portuguese gastronomy and nouvelle cuisine. Lunchtime buffet (except Sat), à la carte 16–20 €.

Portugalia/Espelho d'Agua (A A4)
→ *Av de Brasília, 1300*
Tel. 21 301 7373
Lunch: Mon-Fri 12.30–3pm
Dinner: Mon-Sat 7.30–10.30pm

This elegant building, shaped like a liner, has a circular glazed dining room with a view of the Padrão dos Descobrimentos. Fresh *mariscos* (seafood, sold by the weight) and other fish (raw or cooked): fillet of salmon with fresh spinach, fish soup, fish of the day. À la carte 20 €.

Mercado do Peixe
(A B1)
→ *Estrada Casal Pedro Teixeira, 1400*
Tel. 21 363 6942
Tue-Sat noon–4pm, 7.30–11pm; Sun noon–4pm
This former fish market, converted into a restaurant, has retained the lively atmosphere of Lisbon's markets: an upbeat mood and diners can choose their own fish or seafood, most of which proceed directly from the huge aquarium at the large barbecue at the center of the dining room! Excellent food, reflected in the prices.
À la carte 27.45 €.

CAFÉS, PATISSERIES

Queijadas de Belém
(A C3)
→ *Rua de Belém, 1*
Tel. 21 363 0034
Daily 6–1am

The place for a delicious afternoon tea or a break after emerging from the Museu dos Coches. As soon as the sun is up, people head for the shady terrace or withdraw to the large dining room tiled with azulejos. Hot dishes (breakfast and dinner), assorted pastries and drinks (soft or alcoholic). Fresh orange 1.50 €, pastry 0.75 €.

Antiga Confeitaria de Belém (A C3)
→ *Rua de Belém, 84-92*
Tel. 21 363 7423
Daily 8am–midnight
This pastry shop is a Lisboan institution. For over 100 years, people have been coming here to treat themselves to the unforgettable *pasteis de Belém* (small flaky pastries filled with crème brûlée). Served warm and sprinkled with cinnamon, they simply melt in the mouth (eat in or take out). Wines and ports on sale. Pastries 0.75-1.25 €.

CONCERTS, BARS

Cafetaria Quadrante
(A B4)
→ *Centro Cultural de Belém, Praça do Império*
Tel. 21 362 7527
Daily 10.30am–10pm

The idyllic cafeteria in the Belém arts center. Seemingly suspended above the waters of the Tagus, the terrace planted with olive trees, this cafeteria definitely has a Mediterranean air about it and is very popular with Lisboan students who come here to bask in the sun. Snacks (hot dishes and sandwiches), drinks and free concerts in the evening. Coffee 0.90 €.

Centro Cultural de Belém (A B4)
→ *Praça do Império*
Tel. 21 361 2400
Ticket office: daily 1–7pm (and 30 mins before curtain up) / Shows: 11am, 9.30pm. Price 2.50–40 €
Classical or folk music concerts and popular shows in the huge auditorium of this modern palace built on the banks of the Tagus.

Dama de Ferro (A D3)
→ *Rua da Junqueira, 480*
Tel. 21 364 5641
Mon-Sat 10–4am
A product of the Lisboan *movida* scene, this bar was the first to invade the peaceful district of Belém. Eccentric furniture, shiny orange walls, designer lamps: the décor of the Dama de Ferro provides a hip setting for reggae

music and pop (recorded bands, MTV on a giant screen) and strong spirits. Rum, *batida de coco* 3.50 €. Snacks (toast, hamburgers).

SHOPPING

Coisas do Arco do Vinho (A B4)
→ *Centro Cultural de Belém, Rua Bartolomeu Dias, loja 7 and 8*
Tel. 21 364 2031
Tue-Sun 11am–8pm
The best wine shop in Lisbon (1st floor of the Centro Cultural de Belém). Wines, all vintages of port, excellent delicatessen department and everything for wine-lovers (corkscrews, Riedel glasses, wine stoppers, carafes, etc).

Livraria Bertrand (A B4)
→ *Centro Cultural de Belém, Praça do Império, Modulo 3*
Tel. 21 364 5637
Daily 11am–8pm
A branche of the city's oldest bookshop, founded in 1732 by two French brothers. Foreign and Portuguese literature, travel guides, children's books, fine books etc. on the shelves, and a comfy sofa for consulting the volumes in situ.

AVENIDA DA PONTE

HOSPITAL EGAS MONIZ

STO. AMARO

SANTO AMARO

CALÇADA DE SANTO AMARO

TRAV. DOS MONINHOS

RUA JACARANDÁ

RUA ALIANÇA OPERÁRIA

RUA D JOÃO DE CASTRO

R.J. DE BARROS

RUA LUIS DE CAMÕES

GIL VICENTE

RUA DOS LUSIADAS

CALÇADA DA TAPADA

RUA DA INDUSTRIA

R. RUI PINA

R.E. BARRADA

RUA DO CRUZEIRO

RUA DA GUARDA-JOAIS

RUA DO

TRAV. DO GESTAL

R. DO GESTAL

CALÇADA DA BOA

RUA DO ALVITO

ESTÁDIO DO TAPADINHA

OBSERVATÓRIO ASTRONÓMICO

JARDIM BOTÂNICO DA AJUDA

TAPADA DA AJUDA

ESTRADA DA ESTRANGEIRA DE CIMA

ESTRADA DO ALVITO

F · E · D

3 · 2 · 1

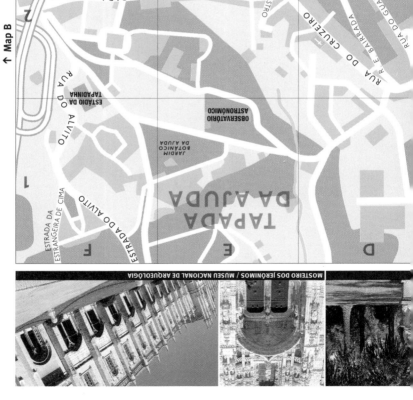

MOSTEIRO DOS JERÓNIMOS / MUSEU NACIONAL DE ARQUEOLOGIA

FERREIRA · PINTO · ORA · RU·

FEIRA INTERNACIONAL DE LISBOA

Pr. das Indústrias

DA JUNQUEIRA

AVENIDA DA ÍNDIA

AVENIDA DE BRASÍLIA

PONTE 25 DE ABRIL

RIO TEJO

0   150   300 m

D   E   F

DOS DESCOBRIMENTOS

MUSEU NACIONAL DE ARTE POPULAR

TORRE DE BELÉM

g the history of
al from its origins to
d of the Roman era.

seu da Marinha

a do Império
62 0019
n 10am–5pm (6pm in
r). Closed public hols
s illustrating the
of Portuguese
ion, from the Age of
eries to the present.

**tro Cultural
ém (A** B4)
a do Império
61 2400
ons: daily 11am–8pm
ng on the banks of
us, this modern
g (V. Gregotti and

M. Salgado, 1992) was
constructed from rough
limestone. As well as inner
courtyards, staircases,
terraces planted with olive
trees and the Museu do
Design (providing a unique
overview of the major
design trends since the
1950s) it also has a
restaurant, cafeteria, book
shop and two concert halls.

**★ Padrão dos
Descobrimentos (A** B4)
→ Avenida de Brasília
Tel 21 303 19 50
Tue-Sun 9.30am–6.45pm
Closed public hols
This concrete caravel,
typical of the prevailing
aesthetics during Salazar's

regime, has stood on the
banks of the Tagus since
1960. It pays homage to
the Age of Discoveries (5th
centenary of the death of
Prince Henry the Navigator).
Take an elevator up to the
viewing platform to enjoy
views of the Tagus and the
compass and planisphere
laid out on the square in
front of the monument.

**★ Museu Nacional de
Arte Popular (A** B4)
→ Avenida de Brasília
Tel 21 301 1282
Tue-Sun 10am–12.30pm,
2–5pm. Closed public hols
Ceramics, furniture,
basketry, fabrics, tools
and paintings from all the

provinces in Portugal.

★ Torre de Belém (A A4)
→ Praça da Torre de São
Vicente de Belém
Tel 21 362 0034
Tue-Sun 10am–5pm.
Closed public hols
Extraordinary example of
military architecture, built
during the reign of Manuel I
(1514–19) to defend the
mouth of the Tagus. Notice
the Moorish domes,
double-arched windows
and Renaissance loggias.
Francisco de Arruda, a
master of this angular style
of architecture, plays with
Manueline styles and
motifs. Stunning views
from the 6th floor.

Map labels: TAPADA, CALÇADA DA, RUA DA INDÚSTRIA, RUA DOS LUSÍADAS, DOS LUSÍADAS, Pr. Gen. br. De Oliveira, Largo do Rilvas, R. PRIOR DO CRATO, R. JOÃO OLIV. MIGUENS, RUA DO ARCO, R. BOA, C. R. DAS NECESSIDADES, HOSPITAL DA CUF, RUA DO OLIV, R. DO SACRAMENTO R. P, R. DE CASCAIS, R.º DE MAIO R. DE ALCÂNTARA, C. ECONOMICA, R. DA, R. MARIA L. HOLSTEIN, RUA LUIS DE CAMÕES, AVENIDA DA PONTE, AVENIDA DA JUNQUEIRA, T. DO CONDE DA PONTE, C DE STO AMARO, STO. AMARO, AVENIDA VINTE E QUATRO DE J, AVENIDA DE BRASÍLIA, ALCÂNTARA-MAR, DOCA DE ALCÂNTARA, DA ÍNDIA, DOCA DE SANTO AMARO, AVENIDA, ESTAÇÃO MARÍTIMA DE ALCÂNTARA, ALCÂNTARA

CIMETÉRIO INGLÊS

JARDIM BOTÂNICO / MUSEU DA HISTÓRIA NATURAL

★ **Palácio Real das Necessidades** (**B** B3)
→ *Largo do Rilvas, 1300*
The former royal residence with its candy-pink façade stands in a pretty garden overlooking the Tagus. The palace (18th century) was originally a monastery, built in 1742 at the instigation of D. João to give thanks to Nossa Senhora da Saúde. There is a fine view over the harbor and the district of Alcantara.

★ **Gare Marítima de Rocha do Conde de Óbidos** (**B** D4)
In summer, the harbor station of Rocha do Conde de Óbidos (1943) is a popular destination for pleasure boats. Inside, panels by the painter and poet Almada Negreiros (1893-1970) illustrate life on the docks. This area is also the hub of the Lisboan *movida* scene which has been revitalizing the city's old docks for several years.

★ **Museu Nacional de Arte Antiga** (**B** D3)
→ *Rua das Janelas Verdes*
Tel. 21 391 2800 / Tue 2–6pm;
Wed-Sun 10am–6pm.
Closed public hols
The largest museum in Portugal was founded after the 1882 exhibition of ornamental art. On Level One: objets d'art (15th-17th century) and paintings by leading European artists (*The Temptation of Saint Anthony*, a triptych by Hieronymus Bosch). On Level Two: gold and silver religious objects and oriental decorative arts from former Portuguese conquests (collection of Japanese screens depicting the departure from Goa and the arrival of the Portuguese in Nagasaki in 1543). On Level Three: comprehensive overview of Portuguese painting from the Middle Ages to the 19th century. Magnificent view over the port from the viewing platform in the garden.

★ **Basílica da Estre** (**B** D2)
→ *Praça da Estrela*
Tel. 21 396 0915
Daily 8am–12.30pm,
3–7.30pm
The queen invested i construction of the Ba da Estrela (1779-93) t thanks for the birth of son. Climb the 212 ste leading up to the dom gaze out over the Tag its widest here). Oppo the church is the tran Jardim de Estrela (184 exotic vegetation, ornamental ponds, a ancient timeless ban and, inevitably, elder Lisboans sitting on be

B

PALÁCIO REAL DAS NECESSIDADES

ALCÂNTARA TERRA

TAPADA DAS NECESSIDADES

RUA MARIA PIA

RUA DO BORJA

AVENIDA DAS NECESSIDADES

AVENIDA INFANTE

R. DO POSSOSSOLO

RUA POSSIDÓNIO DA SILVA

RUA DA CRUZ

AVENIDA DE CEUTA

ESTÁDIO DA TAPADINHA

RUA DO ALVITO

RUA DO PATRO DO

CEMITÉRIO DOS PRAZERES

Pr. São J. Bosco

RUA AZEDO GNECO

RUA SAMPAIO BRUNO

RUA MARIA PIA

IGREJA DE S. CONDESTÁVEL

RUA AZEDO GNECO

RUA COELHO

R. F. METRASS

RUA SAMPAIO BRUNO

ES. DOS PRAZERES

AVENIDA DA PONTE

ESTRADA DO ALVITO

ESTRADA DE ESTRANGEIRA DE CIMA

RUA SARAIV

RUA TOMÁS DA ★ CASA DE FERNANDO PESSOA

ALMEIDA E SOL

R. F. METRASS

ANUNCIAÇÃO

Praça A. do Paço

CAMPO DE OURIQUE

R. DO ARCO DO CARVALHÃO

AVENIDA DE CEUTA

RUA DE C

RUA MARIA PIA

R. J.

R. DA

PALÁCIO REAL DAS NECESSIDADES

GARE MARÍTIMA DE ROCHA DO CONDE DE ÓBIDOS

Spanning the Rio Tejo, the bright red silhouette of the 25 de Abril suspension bridge serves as a constant reminder of the glorious Revolution of the Carnations. At its base, some of the warehouses belonging to the harbor station of Alcântara have been appropriated by Lisbon's nightlife: in the evening, the *movida* sweeps into the night clubs and restaurants at the water's edge, mingling with alcoholic fumes, tropical rhythms and a river breeze. Crossing the flower-lined streets of Lapa, ancient streetcars rattle as they climb toward the center of Estrela: there are superb views of Lisbon from the baroque dome of the basilica.

COELHO DA ROCHA

CASA DO MEXICO

RESTAURANTS

O Natraj (**B** D1)
→ *Rua do Sol ao Rato, 52*
Tel. 21 388 0630
Daily noon–3pm,
7–11.30pm
This restaurant has an intimate dining room decorated with Hindu figurines and azulejos. Take a short trip to India for a tandoori chicken, a lamb tikka or a lentil massala. À la carte 7.50 €.

Os Tibetanos (**B** E1)
→ *Rua do Salitre, 117*
Tel. 21 314 2038
Mon-Fri noon–2pm,
7.30–10.30pm.
Closed public hols
The best vegetarian restaurant in Lisbon, with a serene atmosphere and an authentic Tibetan menu: tomato soup, brown rice and vegetables of the day, *massas* sprinkled with cheese etc and a wide selection of *lassis* and *batidos* (drinks made with fruit and milk). À la carte 10 €. No smoking.

Coelho da Rocha (**B** C2)
→ *Rua Coelho da Rocha, 104 A-B / Tel. 21 390 0831*
Mon-Sat 12.30–3pm, 7.20–11pm. Closed public hols
Although stylish, this restaurant is laid back and lively. It serves

Portuguese home cooking: rice with rabbit, Mediterranean prawns in garlic, partridge tarts, fresh fish and grilled meat. For a romantic dinner, ask for the rear dining room which is more intimate.
À la carte 12.50 €.

Tasquinha d'Adelaide (**B** C2)
→ *Rua do Patrocínio, 70-74*
Tel. 21 396 2239
Daily 8.30pm–2am
This restaurant offers diners a leisurely look behind the scenes of Portuguese cookery. In the small dining room you can savor grilled baby chicken, Mediterranean prawns in garlic or a fillet of *lombo* while watching the cooks in action. Good list of Portuguese wines.
À la carte 15 €.

Casa do Mexico (**B** E3)
→ *Av Dom Carlos I, 140*
Tel. 21 396 5500
Dinner: Mon-Wed 8pm–1am; Thu-Sat 8pm–2am
Nachos in melted cheese, beef tacos, chicken enchiladas, prawns in mango sauce and several dishes 'para los gringos' – those who can't take anything too spicy. The homemade desserts are a treat.
À la carte 15-17.50 €.

ACA • MARINHA GRANDE • MERCADO DE CAMPO DE OURIQUE

Alcântara Café (B A4)
→ Rua Maria Luisa Holstein, 15
Tel. 21 363 7176
Daily 8pm–1am
Painted steel girders, chased columns, fans: a classic setting with a fashionable hint of industrial chic. The cuisine is also a successful marriage of tradition and sophistication: prawns in lemon sauce, goat's cheese salad, stir-fried vegetables in garlic. À la carte 27.45 €.

PATISSERIES

Pastelaria 1800 (B E1)
→ Largo do Rato, 7
Tel. 21 388 2631
Mon-Fri 6am–10pm; Sat 6am–8pm; Sun 8am–8pm
A wide variety of specialty pastries made with cream or fruit. Coffee 0.50 €, pastry 0.75-2 €.

CONCERTS, NIGHTCLUBS, MUSICALS

En'Clave (B D1)
→ Rua do Sol ao Rato, 71 A
Tel. 21 388 8738
Wed-Sun 11pm–4am
This is an authentic Cape Verdean hot spot. On the first floor, diners can enjoy delicious Mediterranean

prawn curry, tuna steak or fried banana plantains, before descending into the basement to dance until they drop (live music). Smart dress and stamina essential. Cover charge 10 €.

Paradise Garage (B B3)
→ Rua João de Oliveira Miguens, 38-48
Tel. 21 395 7157
Thu midnight–4am; Fri-Sat midnight–6am
The coolest Lisboan DJs in a large stylish hall with industrial décor.

Salsa Latina (B B4)
→ Marítima de Alcântara station, 1350
Tel. 21 395 0555
Tue-Sat 8pm–6am
Invited groups Thu-Sat
The most popular Caribbean dance hall, housed in the east wing of the harbor station of Alcântara. Frenetic concerts of salsa, merengue, descarga and other Latin music (local and international groups). On the 2nd floor, La Luna serves tapas and spicy dishes. Cover charge 12.50 €.

Alcântara-Mar (B B4)
→ Rua da Cozinha Economica, 11
Tel. 21 363 6432
Thu-Sat midnight–6am
Baroque meets electronic

music: house music and concerts by local groups. Entry via the walkway from the Alcântara Café.

Kremlin (B D3)
→ Escadinhas da Praia, 5
Tel. 21 395 7101
Tue-Sat midnight–8am
A temple of dance, situated in a former medieval convent. An unmissable port of call on the Lisboan movida scene. Always packed.

Barraca (B E3)
→ Largo do Santos, 2 (Calçada Ribiero Santos)
Tel. 21 396 5360
Ticket Office: Tue-Sat 7–9.30pm; Sun 2–4pm / 10 €
Musicals and recitals, ranging from a tribute to Marilyn Monroe to melancholic ballads.

SHOPPING

Marinha Grande (B E1)
→ Rua de São Bento, 234/242 Tel. 21 396 32 34
Mon-Fri 9am–1pm, 3–7pm; Sat 9am–1pm
Glasses with multicolored stems, fruit dishes, vases, ashtrays and salad bowls, all made of crystal or blown glass. Something for all tastes and budgets.

Casa dos Tapetes de Arraiolos (B E2)
→ Rua da Imprensa Nacional, 116 E

Tel. 21 396 3354
Mon-Fri 9.30am–7pm; Sat 9.30am–1pm
Rugs from Arraiolos: hand-woven from thick wool, their motifs recall façades decorated with Lisboan azulejos.

Fashion Gallery Atelier Kolovrat (B E1)
→ Rua do Salitre, 169/A
Tel. 21 387 4536 / Mon-Fri 11am–7pm; Sat 2–5pm
A look at the underground Lisboan fashion industry. A cross between an art gallery and a fashion store, this boutique stocks the latest creations from Croatian and Portuguese designers.

Mercado de Campo de Ourique (B C2)
→ Rua Francisco Metrass/ Rua Coelho da Rocha
Tel. 21 396 2272
Mon-Sat 7am–2pm
A popular market: fruit and vegetables, fresh flowers, meat and fresh or salted fish.

Ratton Cerâmicas (B F2)
→ Rua da Academia das Ciências, 2 C
Tel. 21 346 0948
Mon-Fri 10am–1pm, 3–7.30pm
Sale and exhibition of azulejos reworked by contemporary artists (Paula Rego, Graça Morais, etc).

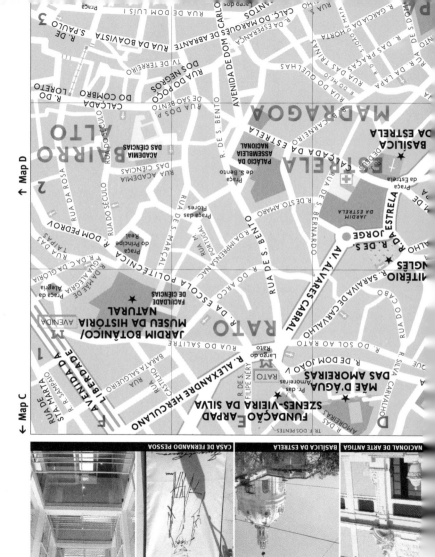

NACIONAL DE ARTE ANTIGA

BASÍLICA DA ESTRELA

CASA DE FERNANDO PESSOA

← Map C
↑ Map D

RUA DE DOM LUIS I

R. DE S. PAULO

RUA DA BOAVISTA

RUA DA ESPERANÇA

CALC. DO MARQUES DE ABRANTE

Largo dos

SANTOS

R. GARCIA DA HORTA

R. DAS PRAÇAS S.º DO MANTO

RCR. DA LAPA

R. DAS TRINAS

RUA DO MEIO

RUA DAS TRINAS

3

R. DE S.

L. DE

S. PAULO

R. DO LORETO

CALÇADA DO COMBRO

DO

R. DO

TV. DE TERREIRO

DOS NEGROS

RUA DO POÇO

DE SÃO BENTO

RUA DOS P.

CALÇADA DO

AVENIDA DE DOM CARLOS

RUA DO QUELHAS

MADRAGOA

BAIRRO ALTO

R. DE S. BENTO

RUA DO SÉCULO

2

ACADEMIA DAS CIÊNCIAS

RUA ACADEMIA DAS CIÊNCIAS

PALÁCIO DA ASSEMBLEIA NACIONAL

Praça de S. Bento

R. DE STO. AMARO

RUA DE S. BERNARDO

CALÇADA DA ESTRELA

RUA DE DE

Praça da Estrela

BASÍLICA DA ESTRELA

ESTRELA

★

RUA DA ROSA

R. D. A. C. DA DAS TAIPAS

DOM PEDRO V

R. DO SÉCULO

RUA DO MARÇAL

Praça do Príncipe Real

Praça das Flores

RUA DE S. MARÇAL

RUA DA PORTUGAL

RUA DA IMPRENSA NAC.

RUA DO ARCO

RUA DE S. BENTO

RUA DA DA IMPRENSA NAC.

JARDIM DA ESTRELA

R. DE S. JORGE

★

AV. ÁLVARES CABRAL

Praça da Alegria

R. DA MÃE DE ÁGUA ALEGRIA

RUA DA ESCOLA POLITÉCNICA

RATO

RUA DE S. JORGE

CITÉRIO

R. SARAIVA DE CARVALHO

NGLÊS

★

RUA DO CABO

JARDIM BOTÂNICO / MUSEU DA HISTÓRIA NATURAL

★

FACULDADE DE CIÊNCIAS

★

RUA DO SALITRE

ÁLVARES CABRAL

R. DE S. SARAIVA DE CARVALHO

1

AVENIDA DA LIBERDADE

RUA DE STA. MARTA

R. R. S. SAMPAIO

BARATA SALGUEIRO

RUA CASTILHO

R. ALEXANDRE HERCULANO

Largo do Rato

RATO

RATO

Pr. das Amoreiras

MÃE D'ÁGUA DAS AMOREIRAS

★

R. DE S. FILIPE NERY

R. DO SOL AO RATO

R. DE DOM JOÃO V

R. SILVA CARVALHO

UE

TR. F. DOS PENTES

FUNDAÇÃO ARPAD SZENES-VIEIRA DA SILVA

D

R. DAS AMOREIRAS

SANTOS

ESTAÇÃO
CAIS DO SODRÉ

EU NACIONAL
ARTE ANTIGA

★
MARÍTIMA
CHA DO
E ÓBIDOS

RIO TEJO

0   150   300 m

D   E   F

4

SZENES - VIEIRA DA SILVA   MÃE DE AGUA DAS AMOREIRAS

**a de Fernando
a (B** C1)
→ *Coelho da Rocha, 16*
396 8190 / Mon–Wed,
m–6pm; Thu 1–8pm
use where Pessoa
r the last 15 years
fe has been the
of the museum of
since 1993. It holds
gs and exhibitions
s on poetry in
and Pessoa in
ar: documents,
ripts and the
bedroom, the only
he house that has
ed unaltered since
h. There is a café
taurant in the inner
rd.

**★ Cemitério Inglês
(B** D2)
→ *Rua de São Jorge*
Tel. 21 390 6248
Mon-Sat 9am–5pm;
Sun 9am–noon
This cool and calm oasis
in the heart of the city is
the final resting place of
many English expatriates,
including the novelist and
playwright Henry Fielding,
who died in Lisbon in 1754.
**★ Jardim Botânico/
Museu da História
Natural (B** F1)
→ *Rua da Escola Politécnica,*
58 / Tel. 21 392 1800
Daily 9am–7pm
Closed public hols
One of the finest 19th-

century gardens on the
peninsula. In the lower
part, the paths wind their
way through subtropical
vegetation. In the upper
part, there are beds of cacti
and succulent plants, as
well as the buildings of the
Science and Natural History
museum (anthropology,
zoology, mineralogy,
petrology, paleontology).
**★ Fundação Arpad
Szenes – Vieira da Silva
(B** E1)
→ *Praça das Amoreiras, 58*
Tel. 21 388 0044
Mon, Wed-Sat noon–8pm;
Sun 10am–6pm
Closed public hols
This former silk factory

houses 81 works by Vieira
da Silva (1908-92) and her
husband Árpad Szenes
(1897-1985). On the first
floor there are temporary
exhibitions of modern art.
**★ Mãe de Agua das
Amoreiras (B** D1)
→ *Jardim das Armoreiras*
Tel. 21 346 6541
Mon-Sat 10am–5pm. Free
The last arches of the
viaduct, adorned with
azulejos, carry water to a
pretty little square that is
the site of the 'mother of
water', the city's main
reservoir. The building
contains the central basin
and a small exhibition on
the history of the viaduct.

PRAÇA DE TOUROS

JARDIM ZOOLÓGICO

★ Parque Eduardo VII
(**C** E4)

→ Tel. 21 388 2278
Glasshouses:
daily 9am–5.30pm

This formal garden was laid out as an extension of the Avenida da Liberdade. On the northwestern side is the *estufa fria* (cold house) with its forest of tropical plants; on the eastern side, the Dos Desportos pavilion with its panels of azulejos. Fabulous views from the highest point in the park.

★ Casa-Museu José Anastácio Gonçalves
(**C** F3)

→ Avenida 5 de Outubro, 6
Tel. 21 354 0823

Tue 2–6pm;
Wed–Sun 10am–6pm

The Art Nouveau house of the painter José Malhoa houses the collection of Dr Anastácio Gonçalves: ceramics from the Orient and other countries, Portuguese furniture and paintings (19th-20th century), as well as jewelry, glassware, tapestries etc.

★ Centro de Arte Moderna José de Azevedo Perdigão (**C** E2)

→ Rua Dr Nicolau de Bettencourt / Tel. 21 795 0241
Tue 2–6pm; Wed-Sun 10am–6pm. Closed public hols

The largest Portuguese collection of modern and

contemporary art, from its precursors (A. Negreiros, Amadeo de Souza-Cardoso) to abstract trends, pop art and minimalism.

★ Fundação Calouste Gulbenkian (**C** E2)

→ Avenida de Berna, 45A
Tel. 21 782 3030
Tue 2–6pm;
Wed–Sun 10am–6pm

Calouste Gulbenkian, a wealthy businessman and art lover, collected over 6,000 works of art in Lisbon from 1942 to 1955. On his death, he left instructions to set up this foundation. As well as Egyptian, Assyrian, Greek, Asiatic and Islamic art, the

collection includes decorative arts and European paintings fr the Middle Ages to th century. A magnificen space is devoted to th Nouveau jeweler-dec René Lalique.

★ Praça de Touros

→ Campo Pequeno
Tel. 21 793 2093
Tours: Mon-Fri 10am–
2–6pm/Tourada: Thu (May-Oct)

The best known Portuguese bullring, in 1892 in neo-Moori style, has seating for spectators. The killin bulls was banned in Portugal in 1933 and

Map labels

AV. CALOUSTE GU

RUA DE CAMPOLIDE

T. DA RABICHA

CAMPOLIDE

ESTAÇÃO

AQUEDUTO DAS
ÁGUAS LIVRES

3 CAMINHO DA

RUA A

RUA D ARCOS

CAMINHO DAS PEDREIRAS

AV. JOSE MALI

AV. C. BO

RUA PROF.

SETE RIOS

MARTINS

R. FRANCISCO GENTIL

2

PALÁCIO
★ MARQUÊS
DA FRONTEIRA

RUA S. DOMINGOS DE BENFICA

RUA S. DOMINGOS DE BENFICA

L.go São
Domingos
de Benfica

CRUZ DA
PEDRA

R. DAS FURNAS

R. CONDE DE ALMOSTER

LARANJEIRAS

ESTR. DAS

JARDIM
ZOOLOGICO

[1]

ESTRADA DE BENFICA

JARDIM
ZOOLÓGICO
★

Largo C. de
Ottolini

1

ESTRADA DE BENFICA

R. CIDADE
DE RABAT

FURNAS

R. D. GALVÃO

HOSPITAL
DA CRUZ
VERMELHA

B

C

SETE RIOS

A

0	150	300 m

PARQUE EDUARDO VII

CASA-MUSEU JOSÉ ANASTÁCIO GONÇALVES

CENTRO DE ARTE MODERNA J. DE AZEVEDO PE

Sprawling avenues bordered with luxury hotels, offices and dwellings extend modern Lisbon to the north. The Avenida Augusto de Aguiar makes its way from the rectilinear Parque Eduardo VII toward the Gulbenkian Foundation, a dynamic cultural complex with mazes of tree-lined paths, open-air sculptures, an exhibition hall, a museum of modern art and a concert hall. The massive silhouette of the Praça de Touros in the east is a reminder of exuberant ancestral pastimes while, in the west, the unspoiled Parque de Monsanto, Lisbon's main park, slopes down toward the banks of the Tagus.

BALCÃO DO MARQUÊS

O FUNIL

RESTAURANTS

Balcão do Marquês (C F4)
→ *Av Duque de Loulé, 119*
Tel. 21 354 5086 / Mon-Fri
7am–9pm (Sat 3pm)
Situated beneath the Communist Party offices, this restaurant can often be crowded out at lunchtimes. Menu of the day (including starter, meat dish and dessert), sandwiches, soups, fried fish, homemade tarts and cakes, served any time. Very pleasant terrace in summer. À la carte 5 €; pastries 1.25–2 €.

Ser-Veja-Ria (C F1)
→ *Avenida João XXI, 80*
Tel. 21 796 1842
Daily noon–3.30pm, 7pm–midnight (1am Fri-Sat)
This bright, modern establishment faithfully follows in the tradition of the *cervejarias*: beer halls doubling as restaurants specializing in fish, seafood and beer. Assorted starters tempt the young crowd (soft cheese salad, prawns), grilled fish and meat and several homemade pasta dishes. À la carte 12.50 €, large beer 1.55 €/25 cl.

Li Yuan (C F3)
→ *Rua Viriato, 23 A-B*
Tel. 21 357 7740
Daily noon–2.30pm, 7–10.30pm
One of the best examples of Chinese cuisine in the city, served in an elegant Asiatic-style dining-room, with ancient pottery and screens. Spicy soups, Peking duck, Mediterranean prawn curry and many other classics. Set menu 12.50 €; à la carte 15 €.

O Funil (C F2)
→ *Av Elias Garcia, 82 A*
Tel. 21 796 6007
Mon-Sat noon–3.30pm, 7–10.30pm; Sun noon–3.30pm
Behind the frosted glass window of this elegant restaurant stands a giant funnel *(funil)* filled with dried flowers. The chef's famous specialty is the *bacalhau do Funil*, a delicious cheesy cod dish baked in the oven. The restaurant also serves meat dishes, grilled fish and homemade desserts. À la carte 15 €.

Poleiro (C F1)
→ *Rua Entrecampos, 30 A*
Tel. 21 797 6265
Mon-Fri 12.15–3pm, 7.15–11pm (4pm Sat)
Fried eggplant, Mediterranean prawn *açorda*, octopus salad and countless fish and grilled meat dishes in this

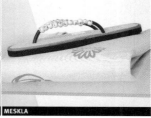

ARIA VERSAILLES MONUMENTAL MESKLA

family-run *churrasquaria/*
rotisserie situated a
stone's throw from the
Praça de Touros.
À la carte 15-17.50 €

Papagaio da Serafina
(C A3)
→ *Parque Recreativo do
Alto da Serafina, 1070-257*
Tel. 21 774 2888 / Daily
12.30–3.30pm, 8–11pm
A glass and metal
pavilion on the edge of
the Parque Recreativo da
Serafina, serving rich and
sophisticated Portuguese
cuisine: Atlantic fish
soup, partridges with
clams in a Madeira wine
sauce, tender kid cooked
in a wood-fired oven.
Attentive service.
À la carte 25 €.

PATISSERIES

Pastelaria Versailles
(C F3)
→ *Avenida República, 15 A*
Tel. 21 354 6340/355 5344
Daily 7.30am–10pm
Elegance goes hand-in-
hand with fine food in
this vast *pastelaria* which
is nearly a century old.
Take your pick from
countless mouthwatering
homemade specialties –
pastries with fruit, cream,
chocolate, etc – while
gazing at the high stucco
ceilings adorned with

chandeliers. There is
also a restaurant area.
Pastry 0.50–1 €.

BARS, MOVIES, CONCERTS, BALLET

The Panorama Bar (C E3)
→ *Lisboa Sheraton Hotel,
Rua Latino Coelho, 1*
Tel. 21 357 5757
Daily 6pm–2am
Take the lift to enjoy a
panoramic aperitif.
Perched on the 31st floor
of the Lisboa Sheraton,
the bar affords breath-
taking views across
Lisbon's seven hills as
well as the Sea of Straw.
Whisky 5 €.

Monumental (C F3)
→ *Av. Praia da Vitória, 71*
Reservations: Tel. 21 314
2223. Information: Tel. 21
314 2222. Ticket Office:
daily 10.40am–12.40am.
Seats 3.50-4.50 €.
One of the largest
multiplexes in Lisbon, at
the exit of the Saldanha
subway station.
Sophisticated sound and
projection systems for an
eclectic program – from
films *d'auteur* to the
latest Hollywood movies.

**Fundação Calouste
Gulbenkian (C** E2)
→ *Av. de Berna, 45 A*
Tel. 21 782 3000
Shows: 7pm, 8pm, 9pm

(matinee 4pm).
Seats: 10–25 €.
Classical concerts, ballets,
contemporary music,
open-air jazz and 20th-
century Portuguese music
are held in Portugal's
biggest cultural forum.

SHOPPING

Adolpho Dominguez
(C F3)
→ *Edifício Atrium Saldanha,
Praça Duque de Saldanha,
1* Tel. 21 315 7247
Daily 10am–11pm
From cotton or denim
sportswear to smart suits:
the Spanish stylist
dresses both sexes for
all occasions.

**Amoreiras Shopping
Center (C** C4)
→ *Av. Eng. Duarte Pacheco,
1070 /* Tel. 21 381 0240
Daily 10am–midnight
Closed Christmas and
New Year
Like a city within a city,
this immense postmodern
edifice houses some 400
stores and restaurants on
four levels. Clothes,
beauty, décor, hi-fi...
there are any number of
temptations for credit
card junkies.

Pull and Bear
→ Tel. 21 386 2258
Fashionable streetwear for
young men and women.

**Centro Comercial
do Céu Aberto (C** D2)
→ *Praça de Espanha*
Mon-Sat 9am–7pm
In the cheerful hubbub of
this 'open-air shopping
mall' you can find
luggage stalls next to
vendors of sunglasses
and cassettes of African
music. Join the regulars at
the bar of one of the
makeshift refreshment
stalls for a coffee or a
sandwich when you need
a breather.

Livraria Municipal (C F2)
→ *Av República, 21 A*
Tel. 21 353 0522
Mon-Fri 10am–7pm;
Sat 10am–1pm
The Câmara Municipal's
elegant official bookshop
stocks travel guides,
maps, history books
about monuments and
every imaginable
publication about the city
of Lisbon. Informative
staff and the opportunity
to consult a book without
actually buying it.

Meskla (C F2)
→ *Av Elias Garcia, 133 A*
Tel. 21 782 6900
Mon-Sat 10am–7.30pm
Portuguese designs and
bright young fashions for
women: colored leather
jackets, flared pants, skirt
and trouser suits with
matching accessories.

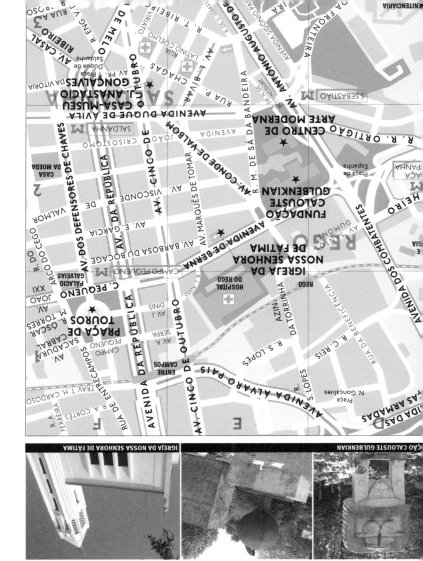

IO MARQUÊS DA FRONTEIRA

PARQUE FLORESTAL DE MONSANTO

AQUEDUTO DAS ÁGUAS LIVRES

---

ced by the more
ine *pega*: the eight
dos (stoppers) form
opposite the bull
tare down the animal
they must then
bilize in the space
eral seconds.

**eja da Nossa
ora de Fátima (C** E2)
*nida Marquês
nar
*.30am–1pm, 4.30–
Free

st example of
n religious
cture in Portugal
8). Inside, the
d-glass windows by
a Negreiros create a
g interplay of light.

★ Jardim Zoológico
(C B1)
→ *Estrada de Benfica, 158
Tel. 21 723 2900
Winter: daily 10am–6pm
(8pm in summer)*
This zoo has over 2,000
animals and 380 species.
Other attractions include
a cable car which affords
a bird's eye view of the zoo.

★ Palácio Marquês da
Fronteira **(C** A2)
→ *Largo São Domingos de
Benfica, 1 / Tel. 21 778 2023
Guided tours: June-Sep:
Mon-Sat 10.30am, 11am,
11.30am, noon / Oct-May:
Mon-Sat 11am, noon.
Closed public hols.*
The walls of the hunting

---

lodge (17th century) are
adorned with angels and
demons, cats and monkeys
with human expressions,
and a bizarre bestiary
combining elements that
are sacred and profane,
impudent and provocative.
Make a point of seeing the
battle room (panels
depicting scenes from the
war of Restoration) and the
dining-room (17th-century
Delft tiles).

★ Parque Florestal de
Monsanto **(C** A4)
→ *Daily/Free*
An oasis of greenery, this
park was created in 1934 by
Salazar. Eucalyptus trees,
plane trees, oaks and

---

cedars cover 1483 acres of
a park so vast that many
areas have been allowed to
grow wild. A telescope from
the panoramic restaurant
affords a view of the south
bank of the Tagus, the
Ponte 25 de Abril and the
statue of Cristo Rei.

★ Aqueduto das Águas
Livres **(C** B3)
→ *Calçada da Quintinha
Tel. 21 815 3630 /March-Nov:
Mon-Sat 10am–6pm*
The Águas Livres aqueduct,
built on the orders of João V
(1729–49) to supply the
city with water, stretches
for over 37 miles above the
north of Lisbon and
Monsanto park.

IGREJA DO CARMO/
MUSEU ARQUEOLÓGICO

IGREJA DA NOSSA SENHORA
DE LORETO

0   75   150 m

A   B

★ Praça dos Restauradores (D D2)

This square is the point where the old city (Rossio) meets the Marquês de Pombal's new city (Avenida da Liberdade). At its center, an obelisk (1886) commemorates the revolt of 1640 which liberated Portugal from 60 years of Spanish rule. To the southwest (Largo D. João da Câmara), the neo-Manueline building of the Estação do Rossio has attractive horseshoe-shaped gates. The start of the Avenida da Liberdade is to the west of the square; the sidewalk cafés are perfect for people-watching.

★ Miradouro de São Pedro de Alcântara (D C3)

→ Rua São Pedro de Alcântara

The funicular railroad of Calçada da Glória climbs to the upper city (Bairro Alto). Here are idyllic gardens around a small lake and a breathtaking view over the *Restauradores*, the Rossio, the Avenida da Liberdade, the Castelo de São Jorge and the districts of Graça, Mouraria and Alfama.

★ Igreja de São Roque (D C3)

→ Largo Trindade Coelho
Tel. 21 323 5381
Tue-Sun 10am–5pm
Closed public hols

The construction of this church in 1556 put the finishing touch to the Bairro Alto district. The geometrical design of its façade (Filippo Terzi, 1575) is paired with a lavish interior: Italianate paintings, altar screens made of gilded carved wood and azulejos. Its crowning glory is the baroque chapel of São Baptista (lapis lazuli, alabaster, amethysts and Carrara marble). Built in Rome at the request of João V, it was dismantled, transported to Lisbon and rebuilt in 1747. The adjoining museum holds a remarkable collection of mid 18th-century sacred ar

★ Igreja do Carmo/ Museu Arqueológic

→ Largo do Carmo
Tel. 21 346 0473
Mon-Sat 10am–5.50pr

The roofless Gothic remains (1389) of the Carmelite convent are moving reminder of medieval Lisbon, whi was destroyed by the earthquake of 1755. S adjoining archeologic museum.

★ Igreja da Nossa Senhora de Loreto

→ Rua da Misericórdi
Daily 7am–12.30pm,
The original church (·razed to the ground

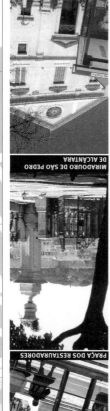

IGREJA DE SÃO ROQUE

MIRADOURO DE SÃO PEDRO DE ALCÂNTARA

PRAÇA DOS RESTAURADORES

Map C →

Restauradores / Bairro Alto / Chiado

The Praça dos Restauradores, a large rectangular esplanade north of the Baixa, marks the border with modern Lisbon. The Avenida da Liberdade, a stately avenue lined with luxury stores, heads north from here. To the west, the narrow Calçada da Gloria climbs through the Bairro Alto to the Miradouro de São Pedro de Alcântara: a final view over the Baixa and the medieval silhouette of the Castelo de São Jorge. Further south, the majestic bourgeois residences of the Chiado, their façades covered in azulejos, lead down towards the Sea of Straw as far as the Cais do Sodré railroad and harbor station.

BOTA ALTA

A BRASILEIRA

RESTAURANTS

Bota Alta (**D** C3)
→ *Travessa da Queimada, 35-37 / Tel. 21 342 7959*
Mon–Fri noon–2.30pm, 7–10.30pm; Sat 7–10.30pm
A Mediterranean feel, with Grecian blue walls decorated with a string of gaily colored pictures. Dishes include fresh fish (delicious grilled swordfish, braised cod), melon and ham, octopus. One dessert you must try is the cake made with almonds, cream, eggs and dates. À la carte 12 €.

1° de Maio (**D** C4)
→ *Rua da Atalaia, 8*
Tel. 21 342 6840
Mon–Sat noon–3pm, 7–10.30pm
This popular restaurant at the bottom of the Rua da Atalia serves dishes like grilled sole and *açorda* (soup made with bread and coriander), cod fritters with spicy rice and *favas com enchidos* (broad beans and cooked meats). À la carte 12 €.

Pedro das Arabias (**D** C4)
→ *Rua da Atalia, 70*
Tel. 21 346 84 94
Daily 7.30pm–2am
You could be stepping into the Maghreb when you venture into Pedro's

den. The Arabian-style décor provides the perfect setting for cuisine that draws its inspiration from Moroccan food: *harira* (vegetable and meat soup) *tajines*, couscous and grilled meats... and, of course, mint tea.
À la carte 12.50 €.

Cervejaria Trindade (**D** C4)
→ *Rua Nova da Trindade, 20 C*
Tel. 21 342 3506
Daily 9am–2am
Closed public hols
This former convent, converted into a brewery, is now home to the most popular beer hall in the city. In a superb vaulted room decorated with azulejos enjoy ultra-fresh seafood and wash your meal down with one of the many draft beers on offer. À la carte 15 €.

Pap'Açorda (**D** C4)
→ *Rua da Atalia, 57-59*
Tel. 21 346 4811
Mon 8–11.30pm; Tue-Sat 12.30–2.30pm, 8–11.30pm
This elegant restaurant was converted from a working-class tavern. The cuisine draws on regional gastronomy, but with an inventive twist: *açorda* royale (with crayfish and Mediterranean prawns). À la carte 22.45-27.45 €.

ÑOL TAPAS-BAR

LENA AIRES

SWEAR

CAFÉS

A Brasileira (**D** D4)
→ Rua Garett, 120-122
Tel. 21 346 9541
Daily 8am–8pm
Sitting at a table on the terrace, Fernando Pessoa, sculpted in bronze, scrutinizes passers-by. Painted ceilings, wood paneling and chandeliers make this 19th-century café an institution. Pastries, drinks, restaurant area. Coffee 1.25 €.

TAPAS, BARS, JAZZ

Español Tapas-Bar
(**D** D4)
→ Calçada Nova de São Francisco, 2
Tel. 21 347 0895
Lunch: Mon-Sat noon–3.30pm
Dinner: Tue-Sat 8–11pm
Above the bar there is a garish photo of a vamp in a bikini, like a reference to a movie by Almodóvar. There is a choice of wines, spirits and authentic tapas. Tapas 4 €.
Fremitus (**D** C4)
→ Rua da Atalia, 78
Tel. 21 343 3632
Daily 8.30pm–3.30am
This long, narrow bar decorated with sheets of metal could pass for Nautilus. Sip a cocktail to

the sound of New York rap or Hindu techno.
Majong (**D** C4)
→ Rua da Atalia, 35
Tel. 21 342 1039
Daily 7pm–4am
Lee Tat Khan has recreated the décor of a working-class Chinese café in his bar: faded blue walls covered with posters and ideograms, multicolored Formica tables, pop music in the background and frenetic games of table football. Rum 2.45 €.
Hot Clube de Portugal
(**D** C2)
→ Praça da Alegria, 39
Tel. 21 346 7369
Tue-Sat 10pm–2am
Concerts: Thu-Sat
Jam sessions: Tue-Wed
You are bound to have a good night at the oldest jazz club in the city. Live performances in the little basement room and a pleasant courtyard for anyone who objects to a smoky atmosphere.
Casas de fado
Succumb to the languorous melodies of the Lisboan fado (nostalgic songs celebrating love and Lisbon) in one of the cabaret restaurants in the city center.
Adega Machado (**D** C4)
→ Rua do Norte, 91

Tel. 21 322 4640
Tue-Sun 8.30pm–3am
Dinner-show 27.45 €.
Café Luso (**D** C3)
→ Traversa da Queimada, 10 /Tel. 21 342 2281
Mon-Sat 8pm–2am
Closed Dec 24-25
Dinner-show 22.45 €.
Faia (**D** C4)
→ Rua da Barroca, 56
Tel. 21 342 6742
Mon-Sat 8pm–2.30am
Dinner-show 32.45 €.

SHOPPING

Ana Salazar (**D** D4)
→ Rua do Carmo, 87
Tel. 21 347 2289
Mon-Sat 10am–7pm
Closed public hols
Clothing for men and women by this famous Portuguese stylist who corrupts classic suits, has fun with the slits in skirts and irreverently mixes materials.
Casa Pereira (**D** D4)
→ Rua Garrett, 38
Tel. 21 342 6694
Mon-Fri 9am–7pm;
Sat 9am–1pm, 3–7pm
Closed public hols
Superb retro grocery: compotes, coffees, sweets, liqueurs and other mouthwatering treats.
Celeiro Dieta (**D** D3)
→ Rua 1° de Dezembro, 45
Tel. 21 342 2463

Mon-Sat 8.30am–7.30pm
Supermarket specializing in macrobiotic and vegetarian products, as well as teas and a variety of homeopathic remedies. One of the few places in Lisbon to sell Asian products such as tofu and seitan. Macrobiotic restaurant in the basement.
Lena Aires (**D** C4)
→ Rua da Atalia, 96
Tel. 21 346 1815
Daily 2–8pm
Sexy cuts, knitted fabrics and bright colors in this Lisboan stylist's boutique of women's fashions.
Swear (**D** C4)
→ Rua do Loreto, 11
Tel. 21 342 7337
Mon-Fri 10am–7pm;
Sat 10am–1pm
Wild shoes inspired by skaters' fashions: platform boots, multicolored plastic soles etc. A must for anyone who embraces a dash of originality.
Valentim de Carvalho
(**D** D4)
→ Rua do Carmo, 94
Tel. 21 324 1570
Mon-Sat 10am–8.30pm;
Sun noon–7.30pm
This Portuguese mega-store stocks African folk, rock, rap, jazz and classical music, as well as musical instruments.

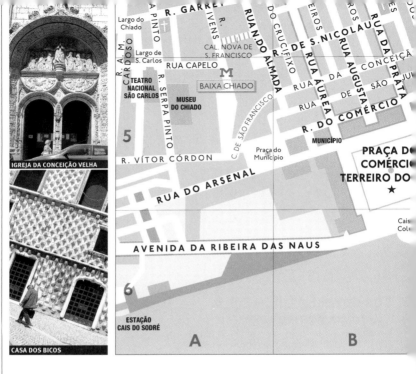

IGREJA DA CONCEIÇÃO VELHA

CASA DOS BICOS

Map labels:
Largo do Chiado · R. GARRE... · R. PINTO · IVENS · R. · RUA N. DO ALMADA · DO CRUCIFIXO · DE S. NICOLAU · RUA DA · A. M. CARDOSO · CAL. NOVA DE S. FRANCISCO · Largo de S. Carlos · RUA CAPELO · BAIXA CHIADO · RUA AUREA · RUA DA CONCEIÇÃ... · TEATRO NACIONAL SÃO CARLOS · R. SERPA PINTO · MUSEU DO CHIADO · RUA DA · RUA DA PRATA · RUA AUGUSTA · SÃO JU... · RUA · DO COMÉRCIO · C. DE SÃO FRANCISCO · MUNICÍPIO · R. VÍTOR CÓRDON · Praça do Município · PRAÇA DO COMÉRCIO TERREIRO DO... · RUA DO ARSENAL · Cais Col... · AVENIDA DA RIBEIRA DAS NAUS · ESTAÇÃO CAIS DO SODRÉ · A · B · 5 · 6

★ **Elevador de Santa Justa** (E A4)
→ Rua do Ouro/Rua de Santa Justa / Mon–Sat 7am–11pm; Sun 9am–11pm
Influenced by G. Eiffel, this neo-Gothic metal structure was built (1898–1901) by R. Mesnier du Ponsard. The elevator takes seconds to reach the Praça do Carmo. Take the stairs to the terrace and enjoy the view over the Igreja do Carmo and the checkerboard layout of the Baixa.

★ **Praça Dom Pedro IV/ Praça do Rossio** (E A3)
Rechristened Dom Pedro IV in the 19th century, this square is still known by its medieval name (Rossio). Before the fire of 1755, it was the site of the city's most impressive buildings. At its center stand two baroque fountains and a monument dedicated to Dom Pedro IV (1870), the first ruler of Brazil. To the north is the Teatro Nacional Doña Maria II, designed by de Pombal's architects. People selling lottery tickets or sunglasses vie with shoe-shiners for the best spot on the sidewalks bordering the square.

★ **Praça do Comércio/ Terreiro do Paço** (E B5)
The impressive baroque triumphal arch (19th century) marks the spot where the Baixa opens out onto the Tagus. Lined with classical buildings and arcades, the most beautiful square in the city symbolizes de Pombal's new Lisbon. At the center stands the equestrian statue of João I (1775) gazing out toward the Tagus: the Ponte 25 de Abril and the silhouette of the Cristo Rei can be seen in the distance.

★ **Igreja da Conceição Velha** (E C5)
→ Rua da Alfândega Mon–Fri 8am–6pm; Sat-Sun 8.30am–1pm
A stone's throw from the elegant arcades of the Praça do Comércio, de Pombal's stark estheti... meet the exuberance o... Manueline ornamenta... The intricately worked façade of this church i... of the few elements o... original building (152c... survived the earthqua...

★ **Casa dos Bicos** (E...
→ Rua dos Bacalhoeir... Campo das Cebolas / S... Tel. 21 881 0900 Mon-Fri 9.30am–5pm.
This unusual architec... sight is the legacy of a... wealthy merchant wh... keen to make his mar... the banks of the Tagu... was the custom in the...

E

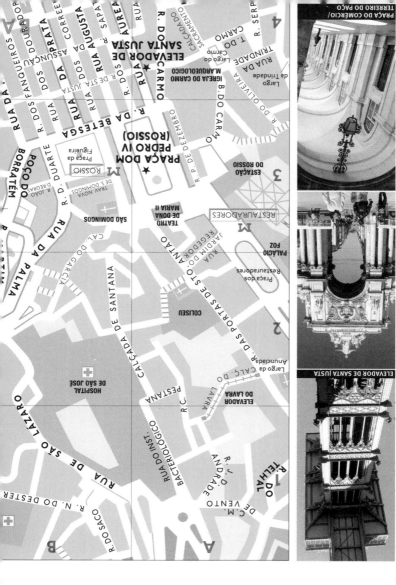

PRAÇA DO COMÉRCIO/
TERREIRO DO PAÇO

ELEVADOR DE SANTA JUSTA

RUA DA
DOS FANQUEIROS
R. DOS CORREEI
ASSUNÇÃO
R. DA PRATA
R. AUREA
R. DOS SAPAT
R. DA
CALÇADADO
SACRAMENTO
R. SERP

ELEVADOR DE
SANTA JUSTA

ELEVADOR DE
SANTA JUSTA

RUA DO CARMO

R. DR. DE STA. JUSTA

RUA DA BETESGA

R. DO
CARMO

T. DO
CARMO

RUA DA
TRINDADE

Largo do
Carmo

IGREJA DO CARMO
M.ARQUEOLOGICO

Largo
da Trindade

R. DO OLIVEIRA

BORRATÉM

POÇO DO

R. D. DUARTE

R. JOÃO
D'OREGA

PRAÇA DOM
PEDRO IV
(ROSSIO)

Praça da
Figueira

M ROSSIO

★

R. P. DE DEZEMBRO

RUA DA PALMA

CAL. DO GARCIA

TRAV. NOVA
DE S. DOMINGOS

SÃO DOMINGOS

TEATRO
DE DONA
MARIA II

JARDIM DO
REGEDOR

RUA DE SANTO ANTÃO

RESTAURADORES

ESTAÇÃO
DO ROSSIO

PALÁCIO
FOZ

Praça dos
Restauradores

CALÇADA DE SANTANA

COLISEU

Largo da
Anunciada

RUA DAS PORTAS DE STO. ANTÃO

HOSPITAL
DE SÃO JOSÉ

PESTANA

RUA DO INST.
BACTERIOLÓGICO

R.C.
DO LAVRA

CALÇ. D.

ELEVADOR
DO LAVRA

R. DO TELHAL

RUA DE SÃO LÁZARO

R. N. DO DESTER

R. DO SACO

R. J. D.
ANDRADE

R. C.M.
DE VENTO

From the panoramic viewing platform of the Elevador de Santa Justa, the 'lower city' spreads out in a harmonious checkerboard of streets, a masterpiece of town-planning dating back to the Enlightenment. The elegant Rua Augusta, paved with dichromatic mosaics, leads to the Praça do Comércio – a spectacular waterside esplanade that is a symbol of the city's past as an influential river port. To the east, the Portuguese capital becomes a village: a labyrinth of alleyways, dead-ends, small tree-lined squares, steep stairways and street urchins. The timeless district of the Alfama is the hub of working-class Lisbon.

CERVEJARIA RUCA

JOÃO DO GRÃO

RESTAURANTS

Cervejaria Ruca (**E** B5)
→ *Rua da Conceição, 47*
Tel. 21 887 9433
Mon-Fri noon–9.30pm; Sat noon–3.30pm. Closed July
You must visit this popular restaurant in the Baixa to sample the main house specialty: Mediterranean prawns in garlic and tender shrimps simmered with garlic and spices in an earthenware dish. You also won't regret ordering the *bacalhau al lagareiro* (cooked with olive oil, milk and potatoes).
À la carte 7.50 €.

Adega Triunfo (**E** C5)
→ *Rua dos Bacalhoeiros, 129 / Tel. 21 886 9840*
Daily noon-4pm, 6.30-11pm Closed Sun from Oct-Feb
Although this restaurant is in the former 'cod fishermen's' street, it places equal emphasis on meat and fish recipes. The star attraction is the *cozido*, a stew made with sausages and aromatic spices. À la carte 10 €.

Adega Zé da Viola (**E** C5)
→ *Rua da Madalena, 25-27*
Tel. 21 887 4202
Mon-Sat 9am–9pm
On the façade, a panel of azulejos depicts a plump monk quaffing a glass of wine... an encouraging

sign for a good blowout! Grilled sea bream, cod in sauce and, one of the highlights on the menu, *joaquinzinhos fritos*, a dish of small grilled rock.
À la carte 10 €.

Frei Papinhas (**E** D3)
→ *Rua de São Tomé, 13*
Tel. 21 886 6471 / Mon-Sat noon–3.30pm, 7–10.30pm
Clinging to a slope in the Castelo district, the narrow glazed dining room of Frei Papinhas extends along the street. Start your meal with mouthwatering small cheeses made from sheep's milk, followed by grilled meat dishes or fish served with sprigs of fresh watercress. Beautifully presented.
À la carte 12.50 €.

João do Grão (**E** B4)
→ *Rua dos Correeiros, 220-226 / Tel. 21 342 4757*
Daily noon-3pm, 6.30-10pm
Sample the *meia-desfeita* (breaded cod cooked with chickpeas, olive oil and coriander) in this great restaurant in the Baixa, popular since the 1960s.
À la carte 12.45 €.

Jardim do Marisco (**E** D5)
→ *Doca Jardim do Tabaco, Pavilhão AB*
Tel. 21 882 4242
Daily 12.30pm–1am
This restaurant amply

...ARIA NACIONAL **CONSERVEIRA DE LISBOA** **MANUEL TAVARES**

meets the challenge of providing a 5-star service at popular beer hall prices. An array of waiters ply up and down the vast dining room with its industrial décor, their arms laden with platters of seafood, crayfish, etc. A medley of interesting dishes and a lovely terrace overlooking the Tagus. À la carte 15 €.

PATISSERIES

Confeitaria Nacional (E B3)
→ *Praça da Figueira, 18 B*
Tel. 21 342 4470 / Mon-Fri
8am–8pm; Sat 8am–2pm
Founded in 1829, the best patisserie in the city celebrates the many types of Portuguese pastries: *queijadas de Sintra* (cheese cakes), *doces de ovos d'Aveiro* (made with eggs). Eat in or take out. Cake 2.50 €.

Pastelaria Suíça (E A3)
→ *Praça Dom Pedro IV, 96-101 / Tel. 21 321 4090*
Daily 7am–9pm
One terrace overlooking the Praça Dom Pedro IV, the other on the Praça da Figueira. This large bright, modern *pastelaria* is in a prime position north of the Baixa. Numerous types of pastry (with cream, fruit, eggs), sandwiches,

omelets, drinks. Pastry 2€.

TASCAS, THEATER, CONCERTS

Ginjinha Sem Rival-Eduardino (E A3)
→ *Rua das Portas do Santo Antão, 7*
Mon-Sat 7am–noon, 4pm–midnight.
Closed public hols
In this cosy bar drinkers crowd around the small bar to sample all types of 'house' liqueurs. The star attraction is *ginjinha* 'Especial': slightly acid Morello cherries in *eau-de-vie*. Alcoholic drinks 1.50–2.50 €.

Teatro Nacional Dona Maria II (E A3)
→ *Praça Dom Pedro IV, 1150*
Tel. 21 325 0800
Seats 7.50–17.45 €
Ticket office: Tue-Sat 1–9pm
(4pm Sun). Closed August
The imposing neoclassical façade of Lisbon's main theater, inaugurated in 1846, stands to the north of the Rossio. It has two auditoriums (Garrett – a superb Italian-style theater and Estúdio) which put on a program of classical and modern drama. There is an adjoining well-stocked theater bookshop.

Musicais (E D5)
→ *Avenida Infante Dom Henrique, Doca Jardim do Tabaco /Tel. 21 887 7155*
Mon-Sat 7pm–4am
Music and strong alcohol on the banks of the Tagus in this warehouse which has been converted into a music bar and is fast becoming a new hot spot on the Lisboan *movida* scene. Recorded or live music (Thu-Sat evening): DJ's, percussion, samba.

Coliseu dos Recreios (E A2)
→ *Rua das Portas do Santo Antão, 96*
Tel. 21 324 0580
Ticket office: daily 1–7pm
Closed August
The biggest venue in Lisbon puts on a varied program of music (Portuguese and international variety shows, classical music, fados). Originally designed as a circus ring, there is still a circus here in December.

SHOPPING

Casa Macário (E B4)
→ *Rua Augusta, 272-276*
Tel. 21 342 0900
Mon-Fri 9am–7pm; Sat 9am–1pm (June-Sep: Mon-Sat 9am–7pm)
A coffee store founded in 1913 on the elegant Rua

Augusta. Coffee ground while you wait, chrome teapots and coffeepots, caramels, sweets and ports, all attractively arranged on beautiful wooden shelves. Coffee 4.20 €/lb.

Conserveira de Lisboa (E C5)
→ *Rua dos Bacalhoeiros, 34 Tel. 21 887 1058*
Mon-Fri 9am–1pm, 2.30–7pm; Sat 9am–1pm
A fishing net in the window of this timeless store indicates the store's unique specialty: canned fish (tuna, anchovies, sardines) in a wide variety of flavors: pepper, lemon, tomatoes... Superb retro packaging.

Manuel Tavares (E B3)
→ *Rua da Betesga, 1 AB*
Tel. 21 342 4209
Mon-Fri 9.30am–7.30pm; Sat 9am–1pm (summer 7.30pm)
Buy the entire range of Portuguese cooked meat and cheese specialties in this 100-year-old institution in the Baixa: *enchidos* (sausages), *salpicão* (garlic sausage), *morcelas da Guarda* (blood sausage with onion, parsley and wine) and sheep's milk cheeses. Cooked pork meats 5–6 €/lb.

← Map F ↑ Map F

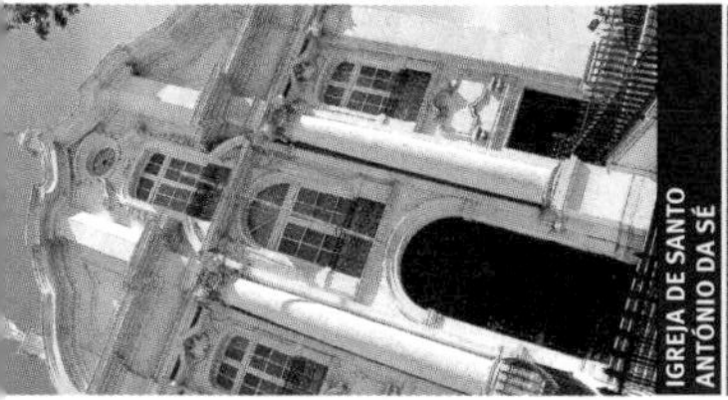

MIRADOURO DE SANTA LUZIA

SÉ PATRIARCAL

IGREJA DE SANTO ANTÓNIO DA SÉ

L. DOS LOIOS

MIRADOURO DE SANTA LUZIA

BECO DO AZINHAL

4

MUSEU DAS ARTES DECORATIVAS

RUA DO RECOLHIMENTO

L. de Sta. Luzia

R. DA MA...

S. MAMEDE

DE STO. ANTÓNIO

R. DO MILAGRE

R. DAS ESCOLAS GERAIS

R. DO SALVADOR

RUA DE S. TOMÉ

3

RUA S. VICENTE

MENINO DEUS

CASTELO DE SÃO JORGE

COSTA DO CASTELO

MOURARIA

T. DAS MÓNICAS

C. DA GRAÇA

COSTA DO CASTELO

CALÇ. DE STO. ANDRÉ

DE P. DE LIMA

R. DOS CAVALEIROS

R. DO TERREIRINHO

R. DA VOZ DO OPERÁRIO

IGREJA DA GRAÇA

Largo da Graça

2

R. DOS LAGARES

GRAÇA

VILA BERTA

RUA DA GRAÇA

C. DO MONTE

RUA DAM. MONTEIRO

TV. DO MONTE

R. DAS OLARIAS

R. DAS BEATAS

RUA DO SOL

R. DO MONTE

RUA J. MARIA

RUA J. DE OBIDOS

RUA DA GRAÇA

1

RUA ROSALIN...

RUA DAM. MONTEIRO

C. DO MONTE

R. DAS. DO MONTE

R. DA BOMBARDA

MUSEU DAS ARTES DECORATIVAS

CASTELO DE SÃO JORGE

The result was an gant diamond-cut Italian in inspiration Restored in 1983, gained its upper nd double-arched s.

ja de Santo o da Sé (E C4)
→ de Santo António 4 / Daily 8am– , 3–7pm / Free
ar place of worship ed to St Anthony of vhose statue, ously saved from hquake, dominates ir. Built in the reign II, then rebuilt, the vas completed in entrance is reached

by a fan staircase that allows visitors to admire the façade. Every year, on June 13, St Anthony's day, the statue of the miracle-worker is carried in procession. In the evening, the narrow streets of the Alfama are crowded with tables and braseros and the festival continues in full swing until the morning.

★ Sé Patriarcal (E C5)
→ Largo da Sé
Tel. 21 886 6752
Sun, Mon, public hols 9am–5pm; Sat, Tue 9am–7pm
Although this church has on numerous occasions been modified, enlarged and rebuilt, it is still the

only monument in the city that dates from the foundation of the Portuguese nation. Don't miss the Treasury museum.

★ Miradouro de Santa Luzia (E D4)
→ Largo de Santa Luzia
This oasis of peace affords a sensational view over the red roofs of the Alfama and the Tagus.

★ Museu das Artes Decorativas (E D4)
→ Largo das Portas do Sol, 2
Tel. 21 888 4600
Tue-Sun 10am–5pm
Civic furniture (17th and 18th centuries), azulejos (from palaces and quintas in the area) and works by

Portuguese and foreign artists. The school (Institute of Portuguese Applied Arts) teaches some 20 crafts associated with the decorative arts.

★ Castelo de São Jorge (E C3)
→ Costa do Castelo
Tel. 21 887 7244
Daily 9am–9pm
Romans, Visigoths and Moors occupied this castle long before the arrival of the first Portuguese rulers. This proud majestic castle dominates Lisbon which is spread out below. It has lovely grounds planted with flowers and trees (species brought back from Brazil).

IGREJA/CONVENTO MADRE DE DEUS

MUSEU NACIONAL DO AZULEJO

PARQUE DAS NAÇÕES

★ **Igreja da Graça (F** A3)
➔ *Largo da Graça, 1170-165*
Tel. 21 887 3943
Mon-Sat 9.30am-noon,
3.30-7.30pm; Sun 9.30am-
noon, 6-8pm. Free
Begun in 1271 and rebuilt
on many occasions, the
church displays a rich mix
of styles: Manueline
(baptistery), baroque (bell
tower), classical (nave) and
Pombaline (façade). Inside,
there are baroque chapels
(carved and gilded wood)
and a choir with an
impressive high altar that
imitates the effect of richly
embroidered exotic fabrics.
The corridors leading to the
sacristy are covered with

oriental-style azulejos.
★ **Mosteiro de São**
Vicente de Fora (F B3)
➔ *Largo de São Vicente*
Tel. 21 882 4400
Daily 9am–12.30pm, 3–6pm
One of the city's most
impressive buildings, this
monastery was designed
between 1582 and 1627 by
Filipo Terzi, in honor of St
Vincent, the patron saint
of the city. Its plain white
limestone façade, imposing
dimensions and somewhat
austere style are typical of
16th-century Portuguese
architecture. The
polychrome marble mosaic
(Our Lady of the Infirmary
chapel), the carved and

gilded wooden altar screen
(Our Lady of Pilar chapel)
and the fine Brazilian wood
floor (choir) are well worth
a look. The azulejos on the
walls and cloister of the
monastery depict historical
and rustic scenes.
★ **Panteão Nacional/**
Igreja da Santa Engrácia
(F B3)
➔ *Campo de Santa Clara*
Tel. 21 888 1529
Tue-Sun 10am–6pm
Closed public hols
An excellent example of
Portuguese baroque,
typical of buildings dating
from the reign of João V,
the Pantheon contains the
tombs of former Portuguese

presidents and celeb
as well as six cenotap
to the memory of fam
historical figures.
★ **Campo de Santa**
(F B3)
This delightful cobble
campo is lined with
mannerist, baroque a
neoclassical building
brightly colored façad
The 'Thieves' Market'
its mountains of bric-
is held here every wee
★ **Igreja/Convento**
Madre de Deus (F D
➔ *Rua da Madre de De*
Tel. 21 814 7747
Entrance through the
Museum of Azulejos
This convent for barel

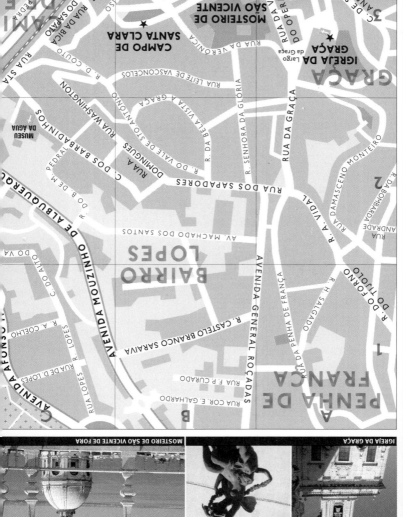

Perched on top of one of the city's seven hills, the *bairro* of Graça is both picturesque and elegant. A panoramic esplanade forms a natural extension of the church, affording an unusual view of the 'lower city'. A maze of alleyways offers a bird's eye view of a magnificent architectural group set against Lisbon's skyline: the massive white shapes of São Vicente de Fora and the Panteão Nacional, which house the tombs of Portuguese rulers. The Tagus continues its course northwest through the city: at the foot of the vertiginous Torre Vasco da Gama, the brand new Parque das Nações presents a spectacular face of modern Lisbon.

LOJA DAS SOPAS

CASANOVA

RESTAURANTS

Loja das Sopas (F E3)
→ Centro Vasco da Gama, niveau 2
Tel. 21 446 2201
Daily noon–midnight
This is a local chain of snack bars specializing in hot soups (with green beans, chicken, beef, etc) and *empanadinhas*, exquisite little patties glazed with egg and filled with chicken, tuna or zucchini. Also on the menu are fresh salads (choice of around ten ingredients), fresh fruit salads and hot sweets (baked apples, apple and cinnamon crumble). Soup 2 €, à la carte 2.50–5 €.

Lautasco (F A4)
→ Beco do Azinhal, 7 A
Tel. 21 886 0173
Mon-Sat noon–3pm, 6pm–midnight
Hidden away in a corner of the labyrinthine Alfama, Laustaco combines a sociable atmosphere with Portuguese regional cuisine. Assorted *petiscos* (various little dishes to nibble as a starter), grilled fresh fish and seafood, pork chops or lamb with herbs. Dine in the small courtyard or in the rustic vaulted dining room.
À la carte 10–15 €.

Casanova (F C3)
→ Cais da Pedra, Loja 7
Tel. 21 887 7532
Tue-Sun 12.30pm–2am (6pm Thu)
This Italian restaurant specializes in thin, crispy pizzas (smoked mozzarella, rocket, zucchini, pancetta, anchovies, etc). The dining room is a rhapsody in yellow with wood fittings and there is a superb teak terrace overlooking the Tagus.
À la carte 12.45-15 €.

Mar de Sabores (F F3)
→ Parque das Nações, Passeio Tágides
Tel. 21 892 2750
Daily 12.30pm–12.30am
This huge *cervejaria*, built on two floors, is in a prime location at the heart of the Parque das Nações and serves ultra-fresh fish and seafood. It boasts a superb terrace on stilts in the water and reasonable prices.
À la carte 12.45–15 €.

Mercado Santa Clara (F B3)
→ Campo de Santa Clara, porta 7
Tel. 21 887 3986
Tue-Sat 12.30–3pm, 8–11pm; Sun 12.30–3pm
Tucked away on the second floor of the Campo de Santa Clara

ESPLANADA DA IGREJA DA GRAÇA

CENTRO COMERCIAL VASCO DA GAMA

market, this restaurant concocts countless culinary delights: sole stuffed with prawns, *bacalhau a bras* (braised cod with scrambled eggs and onions), roast lamb, *cozido* (a delicious Portuguese sausage stew). Homemade desserts and a fine wine list. À la carte 24.95 €.

Restaurante Panorâmico (F F2)
→ Torre Vasco da Gama
Tel. 21 893 9550
Tue-Sun 12.30–3.30pm,
7.30–11pm
The most spectacular restaurant in the city, at the top of the Torre Vasco da Gama. Portuguese and international cuisine, lacking any great originality (smoked salmon, grilled lobster, steak cooked in spices, etc) but always with a 360° view over the city and its river. À la carte 45 €.

CAFÉS, CONFECTIONERS

Cuba Libre (F F4)
→ Parque das Nações, Passeio de Neptuno, 18
Tel. 21 895 8060
Mon, Wed-Sun 11am–8pm
Your eye will be caught by a blue and red sign on the white façade of this

bar that looks something like a bungalow. Sitting on the terrace, you can sip a glass of *cuba libre* or *caipirinha*, while gazing at the cable cars traveling along the Tagus to the Torre Vasco da Gama. Rum 2.25 €.

Casa dos Cafés Portela (F E3)
→ Centro Vasco da Gama, Level 3
Tel. 21 895 1310
Daily 10am–midnight
It's hard to resist the delicious aroma of coffee wafting out from this confectioner and *pastelaria*. Caramels and sweets sold by weight, homemade pastries and coffee ground while you wait. Enjoy them at the counter or buy them to go. Espresso 0.50 €.

BARS, NIGHTCLUBS, MOVIES

Esplanada da Igreja da Graça (F A3)
→ Largo da Graça
Winter: daily 11am–midnight
Summer: daily 11am–3am
By day, this is a small snack bar with a panoramic view of the Castelo de São Jorge, the Baixa and the Tagus. By night, its trendy laid-back

atmosphere is ideal for a drink and for listening to pop music. Whisky 3.50 €.

Lux (F C3)
→ Armazem A, Cais da Pedra / Tel. 21 882 0890
Tue-Fri 6pm–midnight;
Sat-Sun 4pm–6am
The white silhouette of the Lux bar and disco, the figurehead of the Lisboan *movida* scene, looms over the platforms of Santa Apolonia station. In this large remodeled river warehouse, a lavish designer décor houses a mix of live DJs, concerts and themed evenings. Sip an alcoholic aperitif while watching the sun set over the Sea of Straw.

Warner Lusomundo cinémas (F E3)
→ Centro Vasco da Gama, Level 2 / Ticket Office:
daily 12.45pm–12.45am.
Tickets 4.50 €.
This large Warner multiplex screens all the international box-office hits. A handy automatic booth allows you to reserve and purchase tickets in advance.

SHOPPING

Centro Comercial Vasco da Gama (F E3)
→ Avenida D. João II, Lote 1.05.02, 1990-094

Tel. 21 893 0600
Daily 10am–midnight
A shopper's paradise! The superb ethereal structure of this metal and glass shopping mall houses some 200 stores and restaurants, making it the nerve center of the Parque das Nações.

Valentim de Carvalho
→ Level 2 /Tel. 21 895 1265
Daily 10am–midnight
This store, found in many Lisboan shopping malls, sells CDs, from classical to rap.

Natura Selection
→ Level 2 /Tel. 21 895 1358
Daily 10am–midnight
The décor of this local 'Nature and Discovery' store recalls the Ecuadorian jungle. It sells a comprehensive range of decorative objects and clothing from the four corners of the globe: thongs, embroidered Indian purses, linen blouses and candles.

Feira da Ladra (F B3)
→ Campo de Santa Clara
Winter: Tue, Sat 9am–2pm
Summer: Tue, Sat 9am–4pm
All types of bric-a-brac (antique furniture and books, records, pottery, military objects) in this popular flea market, mischievously nicknamed the 'Thieves' Market'.

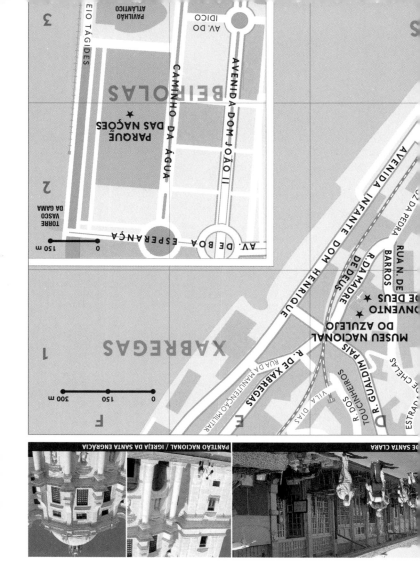

OCEANÁRIO

scan nuns (16th
y) was so luxurious it
have been mistaken
alace. Hard hit by the
uake of 1755, it was
in the 18th century.
urch is a perfect
le of late 18th-century
us art. In the *corso*
allery) is a splendid
d ceiling (Scenes
e Life of the Virgin
the nave abounds
ue and white Dutch
s (17th century) and
and gilded wood.
y remaining vestiges
riginal building are
ster of the convent
h azulejos), the
l portal decorated

with Manueline motifs
(fishing net and pelican)
and the crypt (Sevillian
16th-century tiles).

★ Museu Nacional do Azulejo (F D1)

→ *Rua da Madre de Deus, 4*
Tel. 21 814 7747
Tue 2–6pm; Wed-Sun 10am–
6pm. Closed public hols
This museum presents a
chronological overview of
500 years of azulejo art on
two floors of the Madre de
Deus convent. Hispano-
Moorish geometric designs
(15th-16th centuries), tiles
from Antwerp (16th
century), baroque examples
and contemporary designs
(the most surprising of all).

The museum's star
attractions are the Nossa
Senhora da Vida panel,
a Portuguese mannerist
trompe-l'œil masterpiece
(Marçal de Matos, 1580),
and the immense panel
(75ft) showing Lisbon
before the earthquake.
Antique reproductions
are on sale in the store.

★ Parque das Nações (F F2)

→ *www.parquedasnacoes.pt*
Torre Vasco da Gama:
Daily 10am–10pm / Cable
Car: Mon-Fri 11am–7pm
Far from being abandoned
after Expo'98, the Parque
das Nações has become an
integral part of city life. A

district in its own right,
popular for family outings,
it was built along the banks
of the Tagus and between
the futurist buildîngs of the
Expo. The main attractions
are the Torre Vasco da
Gama (with a panoramic
restaurant) and the cable
car from which visitors can
contemplate the Vasco de
Gama bridge.

★ Oceanário (F F4)

→ *Esplanada Dom Carlos I,*
Doca Olivais
Tel. 21 891 7006
Daily 10am–7pm
The biggest oceanarium in
Europe is housed in this
remarkable steel and glass
structure.

RAILROAD STATIONS

Estação de Santa Apolónia (F C3)
→ Tel. 21 888 4025
Daily 8am–11pm
Trains from France, Spain and north Portugal.

Estação do Barreiro
→ *Soflusa ferries. Free to station (Sul ferry terminal)*
From the other side of the Tagus. Serves southern Portugal (the Algarve) and Seville.

Estação Central do Rossio (E A3)
West Coast (Sintra, Queluz).

Estação Cais do Sodré (D C6)
→ *Departs every 20 mins*
Cascais and Estoril.

RAILROAD STATIONS

RAILROAD STATIONS

TAXIS

Taxis are caramel-colored or black and turquoise for older models.

Fares
→ *Pick-up charge from the taxi stand 1.55 €*
Pick-up charge from the street 0.75 €; luggage 1.50 €
Fares shown on the meter for journeys within the city. Outside the city boundaries, fares are calculated by km (20% supplement between 10pm and 6am).

Radio-taxis
Rádio Táxis de Lisboa
→ Tel. 21 815 5061
Télétaxi
→ Tel. 21 815 2076

CARS

Speed limits
In the city: 37 mph
Outside built-up areas: 56 mph
Highways: 75 mph

Blood alcohol limit
Below 0.05 g/l.

Parking
Street parking
→ Mon-Fri 8am–8pm
0.25 €/30 mins;
2.45 €/ 4 hrs max.
Free at the weekend
Underground parking lo
→ 2.50–5 €/hr
There are only a few, indicated by a blue 'P'.

Towing
→ Reboque Praque do Aeroporto/Tel. 21 840 84
→ Parque do Restelo
Tel. 21 301 6864

Car hire
Mundirent
→ Rua Redondo, 38 A
Tel. 21 313 9360
Europcar
→ Estação de Sta Apoló
Tel. 21 793 3258
Discounts for reservatic made from abroad.

---

flower shop. It has 24 bright, clean rooms (13 with bathroom). The best rooms are those on the 5th floor (view of the square and the castle). 32.45 € with bathroom and breakfast.

Pensão Estrela (E C5)
→ *Rua dos Bacalhoeiros, 8*
Tel. 21 886 9506
This ancient edifice, with azulejos and small wrought-iron balconies, stands next to the Casa dos Biscos. It has 10 somewhat uninspiring rooms, although a few do have a view over the Tagus. 38 €.

Pensão Nova Goa (E B3)
→ *Rua Arco Marquês do Alegrete, 13*
Tel. 21 888 1137
This pension with 43 spacious, well-equipped rooms has two major pluses: it is centrally situated (Baixa) and has an elevator. Its décor, though, has seen better times.
37.40 €.

Pensão Residencial Ninho das Águias (E C3)
→ *Costa do Castelo, 74*
Tel. 21 885 4070
A delightful family-run pension at the foot of the Castelo de São Jorge. Panoramic terrace and 16 bright, high-ceilinged rooms (with or without bathroom). A firm favorite is room nº 13, with its small balcony overlooking the Baixa. Reservation essential (up to two months in advance for peak season).
37.40 €.

Residencial Camões (D C4)
→ *Travessa do Poço da Cidade, 38*
Tel. 21 346 7510
In the center of the Bairro Alto, this small hotel has 16 spacious rooms including some with balcony. 37.40-39.90 € with breakfast.

Residência do Norte (D C4)
→ *Rua do Norte, 123*
Tel. 21 346 5068
This hotel's façade is decorated with azulejos and wrought-iron balconies. The rooms on the 2nd floor offer basic amenities (bathroom on the landing). Those on the 3rd floor are bright and have a shower.
33 €.

Residencial Verginia (D C2)
→ *Rua da Glória, 72*
Tel. 21 342 3743
In a pink building in the Bairro Alto, this pension has 12 extremely comfortable (though small) rooms with bathroom (bathtubs or showers). 40 €.

40 – 60 €

Hotel Portugal (E B3)
→ *Rua João das Regras, 4*
Tel. 21 887 7581
Elegant hotel (1875) near the Praça da Figueira has period furniture, azulejos, spacious bathrooms and all mod cons. 63 € with large breakfast.

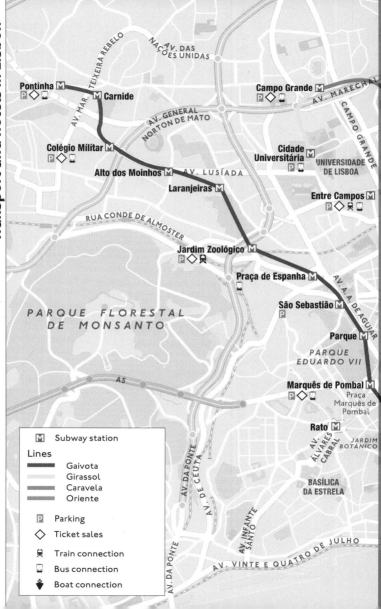

Transport and hotels in Lisbon

Pontinha Ⓜ
P ◇ ▯

Ⓜ **Carnide**

Campo Grande Ⓜ
P ◇ ▯

AV. DAS NAÇÕES UNIDAS

AV. MARECHAL C. R

AV. MAR. TEIXEIRA REBELO

AV. GENERAL NORTON DE MATO

CAMPO GRANDE

Colégio Mílitar Ⓜ
P ◇ ▯

Alto dos Moinhos Ⓜ   AV. LUSÍADA

Cidade Universitária Ⓜ
P ▯

UNIVERSIDADE DE LISBOA

Laranjeiras Ⓜ

Entre Campos Ⓜ
P ◇ ▯ ▯

RUA CONDE DE ALMOSTER

REPÚBLICA

Jardim Zoológico Ⓜ
P ◇ ▯

Praça de Espanha Ⓜ

AV. A.A. DE AGUIAR

São Sebastião Ⓜ
P

PARQUE FLORESTAL
DE MONSANTO

Parque Ⓜ

PARQUE EDUARDO VII

A5

Marquês de Pombal Ⓜ
P ◇ ▯

Praça
Marquês de
Pombal

Rato Ⓜ

AV. ALVARES CABRAL

JARDIM
BOTÁNICO

Res

AV. DA PONTE

AV. DE CEUTA

BASÍLICA
DA ESTRELA

Ⓜ	Subway station

Lines

▬▬	Gaivota
▬▬	Girassol
▬▬	Caravela
▬▬	Oriente

P	Parking
◇	Ticket sales
▯	Train connection
▯	Bus connection
▼	Boat connection

AV. INFANTE SANTO

AV. VINTE E QUATRO DE JULHO

Ca

AIRPORT

Aeroporto de Lisboa
4 miles n/e of the Rossio.
Information
→ Tel 21 841 35 00
Links with the city center
Aero bus n°91
→ Daily 7am–9pm (every 20 mins). Duration 30 mins
Price 2.30 €/day;
5.40 €/3 days
Free for travelers on TAP (Portuguese airline).
Local buses 8-44-45
→ Every 15 mins (3 mins' walk from the terminal)
6am–midnight. Duration 30 mins. Price 0.85 €.
Taxi
→ Duration 15-20 mins
Price 12.50–15 €.

AEROPORTO DE LISBOA
PORTELA DE SACAVÉM
AMADORA
PONTE V. DA GAMA
AV. G. NORTON DE MATOS
AV. M. GOMES DA COSTA
AV. A. GAGO COUTINHO
PARQUE FLORESTAL DE MONSANTO
AV. A. REIS
Praça M. de Pombal
GRAÇA
ALFAMA
Rossio
BELÉM LAPA
RIO TEJO
TORRE DE BELÉM
PONTE 25 DE ABRIL
ALMADA
BANÁTICA
BARREIRO

AIRPORT AND ACCESS ROUTES

LISBON'S AIRPORT

Unless otherwise indicated the prices given here are for a double room with bathroom, including hotel tax. Most of the hotels in the city center are found in the Baixa, around the Rossio and the Praça de Figueira. Bear in mind that it is often essential to book in peak season (July-Sep), particularly in the smaller pensions.

CAMPING

Campismo de Monsanto
→ Estrada da Circunvalaçao, 1500 (four miles west of the city center)
Tel. 21 760 9620
This vast camp site is in the Parque Monsanto and boasts a range of amenities including tennis, mini-golf, a swimming pool, bar and restaurant.
Free for children under six.
4 €/night/person.

YOUTH HOSTELS

Information and reservations
Movijovem (**C** F2)
→ Avenida Duque de Avila, 137 / Tel. 21 359 6000
To obtain a *Pousada de Juventud* (Portuguese youth hostel) card.
Pousada de Juventud (**C** F3)
→ Rua Andrade Corvo, 46
Tel. 21 353 2696
This hostel near the Casal Ribeiro bus station offers 200 beds in comfortable surroundings at reasonable prices.
Dormitory 10 €/ person, double 25 €.
Pousada Parque das Nações
→ Rua de Moscavide, 47-101 / Tel. 21 892 0890
Comfort and modernity at the heart of the futurist Parque das Nações.
Rooms for 2 or 4 people.
Laundry and disabled

access. 8.50 €/person in the dormitory; 20 € for a double.

UNDER 30 €

Pensão Arco Bandeira (**E** B4)
→ Rua dos Sapateiros, 226
Tel. 21 342 3478
A charmingly retro family-run pension south of the Rossio, with 1950s furniture and an old wooden radio in the lobby. It has 12 spotless rooms including 2 with a small balcony. Toilets and shower on the landing.
27 –30 €.
Pensão Varandas (**E** C5)
→ Rua dos Bacalhoeiros, 8
Tel. 21 887 0519
A delightful pension at the junction of the Baixa and the Alfama offering 13 spotless rooms of all sizes and to suit all budgets.
N° 3 (large double room with shower and small

balcony overlooking the Tagus) is particularly attractive. 20–30 €
Residencial Iris (**D** C2)
→ Rua da Glória, 2 A
Tel. 21 342 3157
A popular pension near the Restauradores with 9 quaint rooms. 25 €.

30 – 40 €

Pensão Beira-Mar (**E** D4)
→ Largo Terreiro do Trigo, 16
Tel. 21 886 9933
This pension is on the 5th floor of a handsome building covered with azulejos overlooking the Tagus: 10 bright rooms with high ceilings (some have a small balcony and view over the Tagus).
29.95-39.90 €.
Pensão Beira Minho (**E** B3)
→ Praça da Figueira, 6
Tel. 21 46 1846
The entrance to this pension is through a

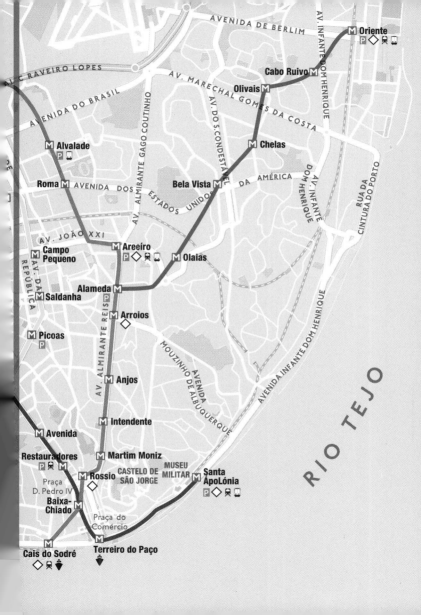

PRAÇA DOS RESTAURADORES

furniture, floral fabrics and drapes). The hotel offers 29 rooms, a bar and its own private garden for breakfasting in the sun. 123 €.

Hotel Mundial (E B3)
➔ *Rua Dom Duarte, 4*
Tel. 21 884 2000
Midway between the Rossio, the Castelo São Jorge and the Praça do Comércio, this large modern hotel has 255 bright, plush rooms (even if they are somewhat impersonal). 138 € with breakfast.

Pensão York House (B D3)
➔ *Rua das Janelas verdes, 32 / Tel. 21 396 2544*
This former Carmelite convent converted into a delightful hotel (marble, polished wood floors, antique tiles, azulejos and period furniture) is a haven of tranquillity and refinement nestling in an oasis of greenery . Some rooms surround a patio decorated with flowers where you can dine in summer. Good restaurant. Book well in advacnce. 184 € with breakfast (buffet).

Lisboa Regency Chiado (D D4)
➔ *Rua Nova da Almada, 114 / Tel. 21 325 6100*
A new arrival in the city center. Comfortable, spacious rooms (some with private terrace overlooking the Castelo de São Jorge and the Baixa). Double from 120 € with breakfast.

Sofitel Lisboa (D C1)
➔ *Avenida da Liberdade Tel. 21 322 8300*
Situated on the prestigious Avenida da Liberdade, this hotel has 170 well-equipped rooms, including 59 specially reserved for non smokers. 225 € with breakfast.

PALACES

Treat yourself to a taste of luxury, if only for a drink or breakfast.

Avenida Palace (D D3)
➔ *Rua 1º de Dezembro, 123 Tel. 21 346 0151*
All the romanticism and elegance of the Belle Époque in this palace (1892), built opposite the obelisk on the Praça dos Restauradores. Luxurious lounges and equally luxurious rooms (82) with period furniture and fresh flowers. 250 €.

Da Lapa (B C3)
➔ *Rua do Pau de Bandeira, 4 / Tel. 21 394 9494*
For a dream night. Perched on top of the Lapa hill, the beautifully restored, 19th-century palace (ormer residence of the Count of Valenças) is set among lush gardens, fountains and streams. Swimming pool. 275 €.

PUBLIC TRANSPORT

Carris transportation
➔ *Tel. 21 363 2044*
Daily 6am–1am
Ticket: 0.80 € (1 journey), 0.90 € (2 journeys)
Travel Passes: 2.30 € (1 day), 5.40 € (3 days)
The Carris company runs the elevators, funiculars, buses and streetcars. Tickets from Carris kiosks or on board the vehicle.
Electricos (streetcars)
Five lines (12, 15, 18, 25 and 28).
Elevadores (funiculars and elevators)
Three funicular lines: Lavra, Glória and Bica. One elevator: Santa Justa (from the Baixa to the Praça do Carmo).
Night buses
➔ *Daily 12.30–5.30am*
Eight lines leaving from Cais do Sodré.
Subway
➔ *Tel. 21 355 8457*
Daily 6.30am–1am
Ticket: 0.50 € (1 journey), 4 € (book of 10)
Four lines: Gaivota, Girassol, Caravela and Oriente. Tickets on sale in stations.
Combined travel passes
Passe turístico
➔ *Prices 8.40 € (4 days), 11.90 € (7 days)*
Unlimited use of the subway and Carris transportation.
Lisboa Card
➔ *Prices 11 € (1 day); 18 € (2 days); 22.95 € (3 days)*
Unlimited use of the subway, the Carris network and free entry to 25 museums in the region (10 to 50% discount on others).

ANTA APOLÓNIA STATION

Rodoviária Arco do Cego (C F3)
→ M° Saldanha
Foreign arrival point (including Eurolines).
Eurolines
→ Leaves Paris at 2pm from M° Galliéni.
Journey time about 25 hrs. From 138 € return
Oriente Bus
→ M° Oriente
Numerous companies operating a service to northern Portugal.
Praça de Espanha (C D2)
→ M° Praça de Espanha
Serves the region south of Lisbon: Setúbal, Costa de Caparica.

PRAÇA DO COMERCIÓ STREETCAR

TRAVELLING BY STREETCAR

otel Suiço Atlântico (C2)
Rua da Glória, 3
21 346 1713
n the outskirts of the irro Alto, this vast hotel rooms) is functional d good value for money. personal décor, but acious rooms ideal for ily vacations.
€ with breakfast.
sidência Roma (D C2)
Travessa da Glória , 22A
21 346 0557
s hotel offers 24 plain, nfortable and well- ipped rooms rlooking the Praça dos tauradores. Balconies rlooking the street on 3rd floor. 55 € with akfast.

– 100 €

el Albergaria da hora do Monte (E C2)
alçada do Monte, 39
21 886 6002

Perched on a hilltop, this hotel has 32 elegantly decorated rooms (luxurious bathrooms with bronze fittings, verandahs). It has a small courtyard planted with flowers and, on the top floor, a terrace bar. 87 € with breakfast.
Hotel Britânia (C F4)
→ Rua Rodrigues Sampaio, 17 / Tel. 21 315 5016
This hotel, built in 1944 by the Portuguese architect Cassiano Branco, is the height of Art Deco elegance. It has 30 spacious, stylishly decorated rooms: matching lamps, curtains and bedspreads, and period bathrooms. 100 € with breakfast.
Hotel Lisboa Tejo (E B3)
→ Poço do Borratém, 4
Tel. 21 886 6182
Near the Praça Figueira, this hotel is a successful fusion of modern comfort and classic elegance. It offers communal areas with

azulejos, wooden ceilings and very well-equipped rooms. 98 € with breakfast.
Hotel Metrópole (E A3)
→ Praça Dom Pedro IV, 30
Tel. 21 321 9030
It was from the windows of this fine 1920s building that the Revolution of the Carnations was proclaimed in 1974. It boasts 36 completely renovated rooms (TV, air conditioning, large bathroom) over-looking the Rossio square. 100 € with breakfast.
Hotel da Torre (A B3)
→ Rua dos Jerónimos, 8
Tel. 21 361 6940
This oasis of quiet and elegance is located just behind the Mosteiro dos Jerónimos. Magnificent marble and stone lobby decorated with azulejos and 59 rooms with all mod cons (some with a terrace). 77 € with breakfast.
Hotel Veneza (D C2)
→ Av. da Liberdade, 189

Tel. 21 352 2618
This huge hotel, built in 1886 on the most famous avenue in Lisbon, has a façade like a Venetian palace, postmodern elements and all mod cons. Its 38 rooms are extremely comfortable. 104 € with buffet breakfast.
Novotel Lisboa (C C2)
→ Avenida José Malhoa, lote 1642 / Tel. 21 724 4800
Near the Praça de Espanha and Gulbenkian arts center, this hotel boasts 246 modern, comfortable rooms, as well as two swimming pools and a bar. 70 € with breakfast.

OVER 100 €

As Janelas Verdes (B D3)
→ Rua das Janelas Verdes,47
Tel. 21 396 8143
An elegant 18th-century hotel with romantically atmospheric décor (including 19th-century

Letters (**A, B, C…**) refer to the matching sections. Letters on their own relate to the useful addresses sections and, where followed by a star (**A★**), to the places of interest on the fold-out map of the area. The number (**1**) indicates 'Welcome to Lisbon' at the front of the guide.

CAFÉS, TEAROOMS

Cafés
A. Brasileira **D**
Casa dos Cafés Portela **F**
Cybercafés
Cyber Chiado **1**
Tearooms
Antiga Confeitaria
de Belém **A**
Confeitaria Nacional **E**
Pastelaria 1800 **B**
Pastelaria Suíça **E**
Pastelaria Versailles **C**
Queijadas de Belém **A**

CUISINE (FOREIGN)

Cape Verdean
En'Clave **B**
Chinese
Li Yuan **C**
Xi Hu **A**
Indian
O Natraj **B**
Italian
Casanova **F**
Mexican
Casa do Mexico **B**
Moroccan
Pedro das Arabias **D**
Spanish
Español Tapas-Bar **D**
Tibetan
Os Tibetanos **B**

CUISINE (PORTUGUESE)

Cervejarias
Cervejaria O Prado **A**
Cervejaria Ruca **E**
Cervejaria Trinidade **D**
Jardim do Marisco **E**
Mar de Sabores **F**
Portugalia/Espelho
d'Agua **A**

Ser-Veja-Ria **C**
Churrasquaria
Poleiro **C**
Creative
A Commenda **A**
Alcântara Café **B**
Restaurante
Panorâmico **F**
Traditional
A Brasileira **D**
Adega Machado **D**
Adega Triunfo **E**
Adega Zé da Viola **E**
Balcão dos Marquês **C**
Bota Alta **D**
Café Luso **D**
Coelho da Rocha **B**
Faia **D**
Frei Papinhas **E**
João do Grão **E**
Laustaco **F**
Loja das Sopas **F**
Mercado do Peixe **A**
Mercado Santa Clara **F**
O Funil **C**
Pap'Açorda **D**
Papagaio da Serafina **C**
1° de Maio **D**
Rosa dos Mares **A**
Tasquinha d'Adelaide **B**
Vela Latina **A**
Vegetarian
Celeiro Dieta **D**
Os Tibetanos **B**

FOOD

Canned foods
Conserveira de Lisboa **E**
COFFEE
Casa dos Cafés Portela **F**
Casa Macarió **E**
Confectionery
Casa Pereira **D**
Casa Macarió **E**
Casa dos Cafés Portela **F**
Cooked meats/cheese

Manuel Tavares **E**
Markets
Feira da Ribeira Nova **1**
Mercado de Campo
de Ourique **B**
Mercado Municipal
24 de julho **1**
Organic products
Celeiro Dieta **D**
Wines and ports
Antiga Confeitaria
de Belém **A**
Coisas do Arco
do Vinho **A**
Patisseries
Antiga Confeitaria
de Belém **A**
Confeitaria Nacional **E**
Pastelaria 1800 **B**
Pastelaria Suíça **E**
Pastelaria Versailles **C**

NIGHTLIFE

Bars
Cuba Libre **F**
Dama de Ferro **A**
Esplanada da Igreja
da Graça **F**
Fremitus **D**
Majong **D**
Musicais **E**
The Panorama Bar **C**
Classical music, ballet
Centro Cultural
de Belém **1, A**
Culturgest **1**
Fundação Calouste
Gulbenkian **1, C**
Concerts
Cafetaria Quadrante **A**
Coliseu dos Recreios **E**
En'Clave **B**
Lux **F**
Musicais **E**
Salsa Latina **B**
Fado

Adega Machado **D**
Café Luso **D**
Faia **D**
Jazz
Fundação Calouste
Gulbenkian **1, C**
Hot Clube Portugal **D**
Movie theaters
Cinemateca Portuguesa **1**
Monumental **C**
Warner Lusomundo
cinémas **F**
Musicals
Barraca **A**
Nightclubs
Alcântara-Mar **B**
Kremlin **B**
Lux **F**
Paradise Garage **B**
Theaters
Teatro Nacional Dona
Maria II **E**
Teatro Nacional
de São Carlos **1**
Teatro Taborda **1**

PLACES TO VISIT

Beaches
Costa do Caparica **1**
Costa do Sol **1**
Districts
Alcântara **B, B★**
Alfama **E, E★ , F, F★**
Bairro Alto **D, D★**
Baixa **E, E★**
Belém **A, A★**
Castelo **E, E★**
Chiado **D, D★**
Estrela **B, B★**
Graça **F, F★**
Lapa **B, B★**
Monsanto **C, C★**
Rato **B, B★**
Restauradores **D, D★**
Saldanha **C, C★**
São Sebastião **C, C★**